The Legal Dimensions of Nursing Practice

LaVerne R. Rocereto, R.N., Ph.D.
Cynthia M. Maleski, J.D.

Springer Publishing Company
New York

Copyright © 1982 by Springer Publishing Company, Inc.

All rights reserved

No part of this publication may be reproduced, stored in a retrieval system, or transmitted in any form or by any means, electronic, mechanical, photocopying, recording, or otherwise without the prior permission of Springer Publishing Company, Inc.

Springer Publishing Company, Inc.
200 Park Avenue South
New York, New York 10003

82 83 84 85 86 / 10 9 8 7 6 5 4 3 2 1

Library of Congress Cataloging in Publication Data

Rocereto, LaVerne R. (LaVerne Rodgers)
  The legal dimensions of nursing practice.

  Bibliography: p.
  Includes index.
  1. Nursing—Law and legislation—United States.
2. Nurses—Malpractice—United States. I. Maleski,
Cynthia M. (Cynthia Maria) II. Title. [DNLM: 1. Legislation, Nursing—United States. WY 33 AA1 R6L]
KF2915.N8R6   344.73'0414   81-23215
ISBN 0-8261-3520-X   347.304414   AACR2
ISBN 0-8261-3521-8 (pbk.)

Printed in the United States of America

Contents

Preface vii
Acknowledgments ix

1. Informed Consent 1
   Introduction 1
   Questions and Answers 3
2. Standards of Care 25
   Introduction 25
   Types of Standards of Nursing Care 25
      Nursing Licensure Board and
         Legislative Standards 25
      Joint Statements 26
      Institutional Policies and Procedures 26
      Accrediting Agency Standards 27
      Safety Standards 31
   Questions and Answers 32
3. Recordkeeping 50
   Introduction 50
   Questions and Answers 56
      The Medical Record Per Se 56
      The Nursing Role in Patient Recordkeeping 65

	The Role of the Individual Nurse in Institutional Recordkeeping	72
4.	**Interdisciplinary Practice Issues**	79
	Introduction	79
	Questions and Answers	83
5.	**Independent Liability**	96
	Introduction	96
	Questions and Answers	98
	The Staff Nurse	98
	The Managerial or Supervisory Nurse	110
6.	**Liability for Actions of Third Parties**	121
	Introduction	121
	Private Employer Nurses	121
	Nursing Students	123
	Questions and Answers	124

Epilogue   131
Appendixes   133
   A: Responsibilities of the Registered Nurse   135
   B: Joint Statement on Inhalation Therapy   141
   C: A Statement of Principle Regarding the Position of the Professional Nurse and the Pharmacist in the Handling of Drugs   143
   D: The Professional Nursing Law in Pennsylvania: An Act   145

Glossary   153
References   155
Index   157

Preface

Nurses frequently have a limited theoretical foundation in legal issues and the practical application of professional liability principles. Many changes in the law have occurred because of changes in attitudes, legislative approaches, and the complexity of health care, so constant updating by professionals is essential. Changes in the laws governing the practice of professional nursing, in individual accountability and expanding functions of the professional nurse, and in the introduction of new members of the multidisciplinary health care team have highlighted nurses' interest in legal issues.

In the Legal Accountability Seminars we conduct for professional nurses of diversified clinical interests, it is apparent that nurses have countless questions about problems that confront them repeatedly in clinical practice. Nurses are eager to obtain reasonable guidelines to help them function in an accountable way.

For the most part, nurses are aware of the fact that they should not carry out an incorrect order.

Nurses recognize the duty of affirmative action to report suspected incompetence of peers and other health professionals.

Countless concerns have been voiced by professional nurses about the appropriate course of action when a physician does not go to see a patient whose condition has changed.

While nurses have gained some independence in nursing practice and accountability, it appears that independence has not penetrated to all levels of actual nursing practice. Some nurses are still being denigrated by peers and supervisors for not wanting to follow every order without question. Not all nurses know that it is obligatory to refuse to execute incorrect orders.

Nurses question what to do when the physician who has the primary responsibility for obtaining informed consent tells the nurse to go ahead and take care of it.

Recordkeeping seems to be an area that poses many questions for nurses. Documentation on the medical record is only one major area. Nurses ask questions regarding the manner in which to document suspected incompetency, inadequate staffing, etc. These questions all relate to recordkeeping.

Interdisciplinary problems are another major topic for thought-provoking questions. As the composition of the health team changes rapidly with the increase of new categories of health workers, the traditional doctor/nurse relationship has developed added dimensions. Nurses raise probing questions about these interdisciplinary issues.

The areas of independent liability and third-party liability have also posed problems for nurses.

This manual is a guide to answering some of these questions, to help the professional nurse make intelligent decisions based upon broad principles, and to suggest when legal counsel should be sought. The answers given should not be interpreted as final legal opinions.

Nurses often call or write to tell us how much of a difference the information we presented at our workshops has made in their daily clinical practice. It is our hope that this resulting manual will prove to be a practical aid for nurses in a variety of clinical endeavors.

Acknowledgments

Special appreciation and thanks are due to my many relatives and friends who have given me lasting support and encouragement through this endeavor, particularly my mother and father, Mr. and Mrs. Richard Maleski; my brothers and sister, Ricky, Danny, and Mary Beth; and Sister Joanne Marie Andiorio, Executive Director of The Mercy Hospital of Pittsburgh.

C.M.M.

Many relatives and friends have influenced my life, especially my parents, Irene Centanni Rodgers and the late Edward Rodgers; my maternal grandmother, Domenica Centanni; my maternal aunt and uncle, Catherine Wilkie and Raymond Centanni; my late husband, Dick Rocereto; my children, Richard, Frances, and LaVerne Rocereto; my mother-in-law, Rosalie Dunn Rocereto; and my dear friend, Father Albert J. Leonard of the Diocese of Pittsburgh. I thank them for the many ways in which they have shown their love and support.

L.R.R.

Both authors are grateful to the Sisters of Saint Joseph, of Mount Gallitzin Motherhouse, Baden, Pennsylvania; for the educations received in the formative years. We owe a debt of gratitude to Naomi Mewhirter, formerly of Carlow College School of Nursing, Pittsburgh, Pennsylvania, for making it possible for us to meet and to present the first of a continuing series of seminars on legal issues in nursing.

Manuscript typing services were done very well by Diane Mikolay, Carole Lassack, Charlotte Berrott, and Kathy Shomo. For their excellent editorial help, we thank Lois South and Kate Maloy. The chart illustrations were prepared by Mary Beth Maleski.

Lastly, a big "thank you" to those hundreds of nurses who gave us the background material to begin the book.

C.M.M.
L.R.R.

The Legal Dimensions of Nursing Practice

1
Informed Consent

Introduction

Nurses often pose questions about their responsibilities as individuals practicing professional nursing in a particular state, or as employees of a particular institution, regarding their role in obtaining informed consent from patients. It should be noted that from the outset the doctrine of informed consent developed on the basis of common law, but many jurisdictions presently have statutory definitions dealing with the patient's rights in regard to consent. Therefore, registered nurses in every jurisdiction must examine their particular states' laws and regulations concerning this issue.

It is important for the nurse to realize, however, that consent or authorization by the patient or by the person authorized by law to consent for the patient must be obtained before any touching of the patient occurs. The signed consent changes the touching from a nonconsensual to a consensual act. To understand this fundamental principle, one must remember that the consent requirement is rooted in the Anglo-American common law tradition of one's right to be touched only when and in the way one authorizes. As a corollary, the doctrine has evolved that, in the absence of special circumstances, an individual who is competent to do so has a right to refuse authorization for treatment, for any reason whatsoever.

A legally recognized intentional wrong to an individual may

result when a person is put in apprehension of a "battery," which is defined as intentional unconsented touching of another person. This kind of intentional wrong may occur even though the individual touched is not actually harmed and even though the individual may benefit from the act. Thus, it can be seen that it is important that consent be obtained whenever the touching of another person is anticipated in the plan for medical treatment.

This is the reason why, upon admission to a health care institution, the patient is asked to sign a general consent form for the routine touching that will be necessary in the care of that patient while in the institution. This signed consent form does not serve as consent for a particular medical or surgical procedure. In some care settings, particularly outpatient departments of doctors' offices, the doctrine of "implied consent" is utilized, and no general consent form is executed before routine treatment is rendered. This implied consent was first recognized legally in the celebrated Massachusetts case of *O'Brien v. Cunard SS Company* [154 Mass. 272, 28 N.E. 266 (1899)]. In this case a ship's passenger had joined a line of people receiving injections, and was held to have implied his consent to a vaccination. It is generally advised, however, that implied consent can be considered adequate only if the patient is fully informed about and understands the nature and the seriousness of the procedure.

In the 1960s a number of courts began looking to the quality of the disclosure made by the physician to the patient. The courts have since treated a physician's failure completely to inform the patient as "negligent disclosure." As a consequence, the doctrine of "informed consent" has arisen. In the evolution of this doctrine, the courts have differed as to standards to be used in determining what constitutes full disclosure to the patient. Initially they looked to what a "reasonable practitioner" would have revealed to similar patients. The trend, however, appears to be in the direction of what a "reasonable patient" would expect to know in order to make an informed decision regarding consent for treatment.

Questions and Answers

For what procedures is informed consent required? This question is often asked by health care professionals, including registered nurses. To understand the nature of the legal doctrine of consent, it is necessary first to consider why consent is required. Many experts hold that any invasive procedure that poses an additional risk to the patient requires informed consent in addition to the general consent. Also, any procedure in which anesthesia is used requires additional consent since the patient should know the risks involved. Any procedure that is deemed experimental or that involves the use of cobalt, radiologic, or electroshock therapy, or any medication that is experimental in nature requires special consent because the patient must be made aware of the particular risks involved, the expected outcomes, and the alternatives that are available. Thus, it can be seen that the doctrine of informed consent applies to virtually any kind of "contacting" of the patient that poses an additional risk to that patient.

On whom does the primary obligation for obtaining informed consent rest? Case law has developed the basic theory that the physician who will perform the procedure is ultimately responsible for obtaining the patient's consent for that procedure. In some instances, the physician may delegate this task to another physician; for example, a cardiologist may delegate responsibility for obtaining the informed consent for a cardiac catheterization to the attending physician. However, the primary burden rests with the physician performing the procedure or ordering the treatment because only that specialist is capable of supplying the knowledge generally recognized as being needed by the patient before giving informed consent; that is, (a) an explanation of the nature and purpose of the procedure, (b) the risks involved in the procedure and the consequences to be expected, and (c) the alternative treatments available.

Some courts have also held that an explanation of the diagnosis and prognosis should also be given to the patient if he or she does not consent to treatment. The emphasis in certain aspects of consent is somewhat different in different states. In addition, some states have supplemented or complemented the case law with a statutory definition of informed consent. It is advisable for one to examine the law of one's own state to find out whether the requirements for informed consent are spelled out on the employing institution's forms in the same language as that of the statute.

Of course, all information given to the patient must be explained in language understandable to that patient. This caution may seem unnecessary, but recently, in two separate studies, it was shown that hospital forms intended to inform patients were so cluttered with long sentences and medical terminology that most lay people could not understand them. These studies also showed that 200 patients who were questioned within a day of the time they signed consent forms were confused. Sixty percent of these patients could correctly describe what their treatment would involve; 59 percent could describe the essential purpose of the treatment; 55 percent were unable to list even a single major risk or complication of the proposed procedure; and 27 percent could name only one alternative treatment (Grunder, 1980).

At least 23 states have statutes that deal directly with informed consent to medical or surgical treatments.* With the exception of Rhode Island [R.I. Gen. Laws, 39-19-32], these statutes fall into two categories. The first category is evidentiary in nature: it enumerates the types of information a physician must supply to a patient before written consent is sought. Pennsylvania, Iowa, Ohio, Idaho, Louisiana, and Nevada have enacted such statutes. It is stated in the Pennsylvania statute that prior to obtaining the consent of a patient for performance of health care services by a physician or podiatrist, the physician or podiatrist will have:

---

*These states are Alaska, Delaware, Florida, Hawaii, Idaho, Iowa, Kentucky, Louisiana, Maine, Nebraska, Nevada, New Hampshire, New York, North Carolina, Ohio, Oregon, Pennsylvania, Rhode Island, Tennessee, Texas, Utah, Vermont, and Washington.

> . . . informed the patient of the nature of the proposed procedure or treatment and of those risks and alternatives to treatment or diagnosis that a reasonable patient would consider material to the decision whether or not to undergo treatment or diagnosis. No physician or podiatrist shall be liable for a failure to obtain an informed consent in the event of an emergency which prevents consulting the patient. No physician or podiatrist shall be liable for failure to obtain an informed consent if it is established by a preponderance of the evidence that furnishing the information in question to the patient would have resulted in a seriously adverse effect on the patient or on the therapeutic process to the material detriment of the patient's health. [40 P.S. §1301.103]

The Iowa statute is simple in form and provides more specific direction:

> A consent in writing to any medical or surgical procedure or course of procedures in patient care which meets the requirements of this section shall create a presumption that informed consent was given. A consent in writing meets the requirements of this section if it:
> 1. Sets forth in general terms the nature and purpose of the procedure or procedures, together with the known risks, if any, of death, brain damage, quadriplegia, paraplegia, the loss or loss of function of any organ or limb, or disfiguring scars associated with such procedure or procedures, with the probability of each such risk if reasonably determinable.
> 2. Acknowledges that the disclosure of that information has been made and that all questions asked about the procedure or procedures have been answered in a satisfactory manner.
> 3. Is signed by the patient for whom the procedure is to be performed, or if the patient for any reason lacks legal capacity to consent, is signed by a person who has legal authority to consent on behalf of that patient in those circumstances. [Iowa Code Ann. §147.137 (Supp. 1977)]

Probably the simplest example of the second category of informed consent statutes—the "cause-of-action approach"—is to be found in a Delaware statute:

(a) No recovery of damages based upon a lack of informed consent shall be allowed in any action for malpractice unless:

(1) The injury alleged involved a nonemergency treatment, procedure or surgery; and
(2) The injured party proved by a preponderance of evidence that the health care provider did not supply information regarding such treatment, procedure or surgery to the extent customarily given to patients, or other persons authorized to give consent for patients, by other licensed health care providers with similar training and/or experience in the same or similar health care communities as that of the defendant at the time of the treatment, procedure or surgery.

(b) In any action for malpractice, in addition to other defenses provided by law, it shall be a defense to any allegation that such health care provider treated, examined or otherwise rendered professional care to an injured party without his or her informed consent that:

(1) A person of ordinary intelligence and awareness in a position similar to that of the injured party could reasonably be expected to appreciate and comprehend hazards inherent in such treatment;
(2) The injured party assured the health care provider he or she would undergo the treatment regardless of the risk involved or that he or she did not want to be given the information or any part thereof to which he or she could otherwise be entitled; or
(3) It was reasonable for the health care provider to limit the extent of his or her disclosures of the risks of the treatment, procedure or surgery to the injured party because further disclosure could be expected to affect, adversely and substantially, the injured party's condition, or the outcome of the treatment, procedure or surgery. [Del. Code Ann. Tit. 18 §6852 (1976)]

It can be seen that this statute establishes the elements of the cause of action based on a lack of informed consent.

To make matters even more complicated, in a legislative response to health care consumers' efforts, many states have established rules and regulations based on the "Patient's Bill of Rights," which includes the right of the patient to be informed regarding treatment modalities prior to giving consent for treatment. Some of these state regulations place on the institution or hospital the burden of ensuring that consent requirements are being fulfilled. In addition, in 1972 the American Hospital Association identified the right of informed consent as follows:

1. The patient has the right to obtain from his physician complete current information concerning his diagnosis, treatment, and prognosis in terms the patient can be reasonably expected to understand. When it is not medically advisable to give such information to the patient, the information should be made available to an appropriate person in his behalf. He has the right to know by name the physician responsible for coordinating his care.
2. The patient has the right to receive from his physician information necessary to give informed consent prior to the start of any procedure and/or treatment. Except in emergencies, such information for informed consent should include but not necessarily be limited to the specific procedure and/or treatment, the medically significant risks involved, and the probable duration of incapacitation. Where medically significant alternatives for care or treatment exist, or when the patient requests information concerning medical alternatives, the patient has the right to such information. The patient also has the right to know the name of the person responsible for the procedures and/or treatment.
3. The patient has the right to refuse treatment to the extent permitted by law, and to be informed of the medical consequences of his action. [American Hospital Association, 1972]

The Rights and Responsibilities section of the *Accreditation Manual* of The Joint Commission on Accreditation of Hospitals (JCAH) also has delineated requirements regarding patient consent:

> The patient has the right to reasonably informed participation in decisions involving his health care. To the degree possible, this should be based on a clear, concise explanation of his condition and of all proposed technical procedures, including the possibilities of any risk of mortality or serious side effects, problems related to recuperation, and probability of success. The patient should not be

subjected to any procedure without his voluntary, competent, and understanding consent, or that of his legally authorized representative. Where medically significant alternatives for care or treatment exist, the patient shall be so informed.

The patient has the right to know who is responsible for authorizing and performing the procedure or treatment.

The patient shall be informed if the hospital proposes to engage in or perform human experimentation or other research/educational projects affecting his care or treatment, and the patient has the right to refuse to participate in any such activity. [JCAH, 1981, pp. xiv, xv]

It is imperative that every registered nurse know to whom the employing hospital delegates the responsibility for obtaining informed consent. In most institutions, delegation is to the medical staff and individual physicians. It is also important for the nurse to know the policy and procedures in his or her institution in regard to getting consent forms signed. Usually these policies and procedures regarding informed consent and right of refusal are developed so as to be consistent with state law. Whatever the procedure in regard to the signing and execution of the consent form, the nurse who attempts to explain the nature of a procedure, the risks involved, or the alternatives available is exposing himself or herself to considerable risk through lack of knowledge required to properly explain these points to the patient. If the employing institution has not already done so, we suggest that the nurse ask to have a concrete, well-structured policy drawn up that clearly delineates the roles of the nurse and the physician in regard to obtaining informed consent. It should be noted here that although neither the institution nor the nurse is primarily responsible for obtaining the informed consent, the hospital does have a role in that it must cooperate with and support the physician in obtaining the informed consent and must act to take steps against any physician who is not obtaining informed consent from patients.

Must the consent form provided by the particular hospital or institution be used in obtaining informed consent? The permit, or the consent form itself, serves only as evidence that the informed con-

Informed Consent

sent process has been carried out. Therefore, an oral consent is just as binding as a written one. However, oral consent is very difficult to prove in court, especially since litigation often is instituted years after the patient was hospitalized. Most institutions have their consent forms professionally drafted after consultation with the medical staff to ensure that they provide for: (a) recording that the patient has been informed of the actual name of the procedure for which consent is sought and that the individual giving the consent apparently understands the risks involved and the alternatives available, and (b) a place for the signature of the patient or the person authorized to sign for the patient. Because of these safeguards, it is usually advisable for the physician to use the hospital's form. Sometimes physicians are also advised to supplement a particular permit or consent form by entering on the physician's progress sheet a statement that this has been done. While there is no legal requirement that the physician use a consent form provided by the institution, it is usually advisable for him or her to do so.

Institutions that are accredited by the JCAH are required to include documentary evidence in the patient's medical record that the patient gave informed consent in writing.

Any nurse working in a hospital or other health care institution has the obligation to be aware of the policies and procedures adopted by the institution regarding the use of various types of consent forms and proper execution thereof.

May a physician delegate his or her responsibility for obtaining informed consent to a procedure to an R.N.? Since most case law and statutory requirements provide that it is the physician's responsibility to obtain informed consent (that is, authorization to perform certain medical procedures after appropriate explanation of all elements required, including the nature of the procedure, the risks, and the alternatives available), it would appear to follow that a physician may not delegate this responsibility to an R.N. Secondly, an additional argument exists that the nurse would not be competent under the professional licensing standards to perform this task for the physician.

For example, it would appear that a registered nurse probably would not have the information or experience needed to explain certain surgical procedures the surgeon would be performing, or all the risks to that patient, or the feasible alternatives available to that patient. In addition, case law exists that indicates problems may arise in making an adequate disclosure to the patient, even when a patient is referred by one physician to another, and the referring physician has already explained the risks and alternatives [Pegram v. Sisco, 406 F.Supp. W.D. Ark. (1976) *aff'd*, 547 F.2d 172, 8th Cir. (1976)]. In view of these facts, it is probably not in the best interest of either the physician, the hospital, or the individual nurse that the actual informed consent be obtained by the nurse.

Many institutions have a policy whereby the R.N. has the responsibility of getting the consent forms signed after the physician has given the necessary information to the patient. It is suggested that, as a risk management device, the physician who will be performing the procedure actually get the consent form signed and that the consent carry the notation that the patient's signature was obtained by the physician.

May a registered nurse witness the patient's signature on a consent form? This question is often asked. Yes, it is accepted that an R.N. may witness the patient's signing a consent form. When the R.N. witnesses such a signing, he or she is doing just that—witnessing that the signature has been written in his or her presence. As a witness to the signature, the R.N. is not verifying what was said or that the patient understood. In fact, it is not necessary that the nurse be present at the time of the explanation, as long as he or she is present at the time the patient signs the form. Sometimes nurses misunderstand and feel that by witnessing the consent form, they are also confirming that they have witnessed the conversation, the explanation, and the patient's understanding of that explanation. This is not the case.

For how long is a signed consent form or permit valid? There is no absolute answer to this question. The consent form should be completed at the time the physician explains the procedure, the risks, and the alternatives available to the patient and obtains the patient's signature. Recording the exact time the consent is procured is important in that it provides documented evidence that the patient was competent, able to sign, and not under any medication that would lead to misunderstanding or nonunderstanding of the explanation given by the physician. This is why consent forms provide space to record the exact time of signing, and it is important that that part of the form be completed by someone who knows exactly when the patient signed.

The form need not be signed on the same day as or the night before the performance of the procedure. In fact, if the form is signed on the same day the procedure is to be performed, a question might arise as to whether the patient was competent to sign or understand the consent given. Hence, the form giving consent for an elective procedure may be signed before the patient is even admitted to the hospital. Please note, however, that it is the physician's responsibility to determine that the patient's condition has not changed to an extent that the risks to the procedure would have increased or changed during the time between the signing and the time the procedure is to be performed. It is probably an ancillary obligation of the nursing staff to ensure that, so far as the nursing assessment process is concerned, no drastic change in the patient's condition has occurred in the interim between the signing of the consent form and the performance of the procedure.

Although there is no actual time limit to the validity of the signed consent form, some experts have stated that consent forms over 30 days old should not be used because it may not be clear that the consent was actually meant for the particular procedure now contemplated. The more important question, as mentioned earlier, is whether the patient's condition has remained the same so that the risks have not changed since the time the consent form was executed.

What is the current standard regarding the disclosure required to assure that consent is "informed?" There are currently two different standards as to the nature of information required to be disclosed to the patient prior to the obtaining of consent. The older "professional community" standard required that the physician disclose those items that *other physicians* would disclose in like circumstances; therefore, expert testimony was required to show that the physician in question did disclose sufficient information to the patient.

The more modern approach requires that the physician inform the patient of those items that a *reasonable patient* would have considered essential when consenting to a particular treatment or procedure [Canterbury v. Spence, 464 F.2d 772, 780 (D.C. Cir. 1972)]. Since it is not always clear what approach a court will take in a given situation, and since the law regarding patients' rights is currently changing, it is suggested that the nurse contact the responsible physician if he or she becomes aware that a patient does not have sufficient information to make an intelligent decision regarding consent. This fact could become apparent to the nurse in his or her communications with the patient or the patient's family. Notification of the physician should be documented in the appropriate place in the medical record.

In what circumstances would a physician have the right to withhold information from a patient? Even though the physician's privilege of withholding information from a patient is seldom justified, such privilege does exist in case law and is even provided by statute in some states. However, the physician who withholds vital information from a patient must document in the patient's record what the detrimental effects would probably be if the information were shared. It is predictable that in the future this privilege will be abrogated even more in view of the current proliferation of right-to-know legislation.

The nurse's duty extends to making sure that when a physician has decided certain information should not be released to the patient, his or her decision is respected. If the patient repeatedly asks provoking questions regarding the withheld information, the physician should be notified of these inquiries and the nurse's notification documented in the patient's record.

What is the nurse's role in regard to proper execution of a consent form? First, the nurse must remember again that, in most jurisdictions, the primary obligation for obtaining the consent and for explaining the procedure to the patient rests with the physician. The health agency and the registered nurse have a responsibility to cooperate with the physician and to communicate any changes that would affect the consensual procedure. Some institutions allow the nurse to complete the consent forms after the physician has explained the procedures to the patient and obtained a verbal consent. It is therefore imperative for the nurse to understand the particular institution's policy and procedure and to know for which aspects of securing the signed consent he or she is responsible. Some institutions permit nurses only to witness the signing of the consent form; others require nurses to take a more active role.

Subsequent to the execution of the consent form, the patient can withdraw consent to the procedure, and this withdrawal can be oral in nature. If a patient states that he or she has decided not to go through with a procedure, or did not understand the physician's explanation of it, it is imperative for the nurse to notify the doctor of this fact so that the doctor may reexamine the situation with the patient. Again, the nurse must document this notification in the patient's record.

In addition, the registered nurse and the health agency are independently responsible for continuity of care for the patient and continual monitoring of the patient's condition. Any change in the patient's condition that would increase or change the risks of the procedure would require the nurse to notify the physician of this change and to document the notification in the patient's record.

What is an appropriate response to a question from a patient who has signed an informed consent form but is now in doubt about whether to go through with the procedure? The nursing staff of an institution and the institution have the primary obligation of continually monitoring the patient's condition and any changes in condition or behavior. Therefore, a patient who has given consent and later doubts the wisdom of having done so would, in effect, be giving notice to the nurse and to the institution that he or she is confused about the procedure, the risks involved, or the alternatives. The appropriate response for the nurse is not to attempt to explain the procedure but to try to calm the patient and assure him or her that the physician who is expecting to perform the procedure will be notified of the patient's concern. As always, this notification must be documented in the patient's record, and the nurse must be certain that the physician, or his or her designee, does see and talk with the patient about this problem.

What is the nurse's obligation to a patient who expresses doubts about the impending surgery immediately before it is to take place? This question is often asked by nurses, and the first point that comes to mind is the importance of the exact time the doubts are expressed. If the patient has serious doubts about going ahead with a surgical procedure immediately prior to the time it is to be performed and the patient is already sedated, the question of competency may be raised since the patient may not realize what he or she is saying. If, however, the doubts about the surgery are expressed the night before it is to take place, the question may not arise. In either case, the surgeon who is to perform the operation should be notified and, if the procedure is elective, he or she may postpone the surgery to allow for additional explanation to be given to the patient. Of course, in an emergency situation, the consent of the patient is not required when he or she is incapable of giving it and no one who is legally authorized to do so is available.

Under what circumstances is it not necessary to secure the patient's informed consent? The primary burden of determining whether a patient's consent is necessary in a specific situation rests with the physician performing or rendering the treatment. However, it is important to realize that in a truly emergency situation, consent may not be needed—in other words, the emergency may vitiate the consent requirement. It would be expedient for nurses and other health care workers to find out what constitutes an emergency situation in their particular jurisdictions. Usually, when loss of life or permanent impairment is an immediate threat if a particular procedure is not undertaken, the situation will be deemed emergent in nature and, therefore, informed consent and documentation thereof are unnecessary. It is also important for the nurse to examine the existing case law in his or her state to learn what the parameters of an emergency situation are and what berth of discretion is allowed to health care professionals in determining whether the situation is an emergency.

Many states give the physician a wide latitude of discretion when a problem involving consent arises after treatment has been given in an apparent emergency situation. However, if the physician has doubts as to whether a particular situation constitutes an emergency, it would be best for him or her to document why the situation appears to be an emergency clinically and whether a second opinion is necessary. It would be in the best interest of a nurse confronted with such a situation to obtain consultation from the treating physician and to have that physician document the clinical reason for the emergency nature of the situation in the patient's medical record.

When should informed consent to a particular procedure be obtained, even if that procedure is to be performed in the emergency department? The fact that a specific procedure or treatment is to be undertaken in the emergency department does not vitiate the need for consent, even though in a strict emergency situation the requirement to obtain consent may be vitiated. Technically, any procedure that is invasive in nature poses a risk to the patient, and must be accompanied by a distinct and separate informed consent form signed by the patient or the patient's legally authorized representative. Therefore, informed consent should be procured before any major or minor surgical procedure that involves entering the body is undertaken; before all procedures in which anesthesia is to be used, since anesthesia presents a particular and specific risk to the patient; before any nonsurgical procedure involving more than a slight risk of harm to the patient—for example, a pyelogram, arteriogram, or myelogram; and before any procedure involving the use of radiation, cobalt, or electroshock therapy or the use of electrodes. Every health care institution should also have specific directives regarding any other procedures for which medical staff may have agreed to require a separate and distinct consent form. In addition, the nurse should know what specific additional requirements exist as to obtaining informed consent for experimental or investigational procedures or medications.

In what situations can a minor patient give informed consent without parental consent? The traditional view on this subject is that a minor patient cannot give informed consent for a specific medical or surgical procedure; parental or next-of-kin consent is necessary before a surgical procedure or treatment may be undertaken. However, over the years there has been an erosion of this traditional view and the various states now treat the consent of minors in various ways. For example, Louisiana and some other states allow minors to give consent for all medical or surgical services. Other states have specifically provided by statute certain rules regarding situations in which informed consent by the parent or guardian is not needed.

Some jurisdictions, through statutory and case law, treat minors as "emancipated" in certain situations. For example, a minor may be considered to be emancipated if she has ever been pregnant, if he or she has ever been married, or if he or she is a high-school graduate. Being emancipated entitles the minor to give consent for any type of procedure. Some states also provide an exception to the parental consent requirement for a specific situation in which the privacy of the minor may be deemed paramount to the parental requirement. For example, Pennsylvania has pro-

Informed Consent

vided specifically by legislation that parental consent is unnecessary for treatment of certain communicable conditions, such as venereal disease, for pregnancy-related problems, and for drug and alcohol dependency problems. Therefore, nurses are advised to look to the specific legislative and case law trends in their jurisdictions to learn what the requirements are in connection with allowing a minor to consent without parental consent. Naturally, in an emergency situation, a parent would not have to give consent for treatment of a minor patient.

There is also a doctrine in the law called the Mature Minor Rule, which states that in certain situations the consent of a minor will be upheld as valid even though parental consent is not obtained or even if the parents refuse treatment for the minor. This rule is applied generally in very serious situations when the minor's life would be in jeopardy if the procedure were not done, or in an investigational or experimental situation. If that minor were considered "mature" for purposes of obtaining consent, his or her consent would be valid and could stand alone without parental consent.

In such cases, the courts would take into account the age, intellectual maturity, and understanding of the minor as well as whether the condition is serious enough to put the minor's life in jeopardy if a certain procedure is not done. For example, courts have adhered to the requirement of parental consent when no emergency is present and the child is of tender age, but they have also held the consent of the minor effective when the minor was over 15 years of age and the proposed procedure was for his or her benefit. It is advised in such instances that the status of the minor patient be fully documented on the record if the physician feels the minor's consent would stand alone.

A serious legal and ethical problem may arise if, for some reason, a minor patient's life is in jeopardy and the parents refuse treatment on religious grounds. When this is the case, it is suggested that the proper course of action is for the hospital administrator or the physician to attempt to obtain judicial clarification through court order or authorization as to whether the advice of the physician regarding treatment should be followed along with the wishes of the minor patient, or the wishes or religious beliefs of the parents. This concept is illustrated in the opinion of *In re Green* [448 Pa. 338, 292 A.2d 387 (1972)], in which a physician petitioned the court to appoint him as guardian in order to authorize a spinal fusion operation to correct a curvature of a boy's spine. The boy's mother, a Jehovah's witness adherent, refused consent to the surgery because of her religious objection to the blood transfusions that would be required. Ultimately, the highest state court agreed with the trial court that the state's interest was insufficient to interfere with the mother's religious freedom because the child's life was not at stake. Thus, it appears that a court would not interfere with a parent's wishes unless the child patient's life were immediately endangered. Should such a situation arise, it is the nurse's duty to make immediate contact with the physician involved and with the health care facility's administrator.

Can a close relative, a babysitter, or a nurse in a health care facility consent for treatment of a minor? This particular problem may be posed to a nonparental caretaker, especially when the minor is being cared for outside of his or her own home and is ambulatory. Often a parent leaves a child to be cared for by someone else, and this person must determine whether he or she is standing *in loco parentis* (a Latin term meaning "in the place of a parent") and can, therefore, give valid consent for needed treatment. The cases that exist in this area emphasize that the health care professional must be sure a valid consent from the parent or from someone authorized to give "substituted consent" exists. Thus, health care facilities should have a clearcut policy as to the documentation of appropriate substituted consent. For example, a policy may make it necessary for the parent to be present and to give consent to the first of a number of regular treatments, but for following treatments a note from the parent authorizing the individual accompanying the child to give consent is sufficient. A nurse working in this kind of setting needs to be cognizant of the particular institution's policy in this regard.

What is the duty of the health care professional regarding information that a minor patient does not wish revealed to the parents? Some states have laws covering certain conditions, particularly those involving drug-, alcohol-, or sex-related problems, which expressly prohibit caretakers from disclosing relevant information to parents. These laws may be based on the minor's right to privacy in situations in which disclosure may be especially offensive to the child. Practically speaking, however, it is unlikely that a health care professional could be successfully sued if disclosure is made to the parent in good faith.

A nurse working in a health care institution must look to the institution and to the particular physician involved to determine what information should or may be disclosed, especially in situations dealing with conditions of a sensitive nature.

Under what circumstances can next of kin consent to treatment, and does priority for next of kin exist? The general rule is that a patient must give consent for the proposed treatment or procedure. When a patient is unable for any reason to consent to needed treatment, the consent may be obtained from the patient's nearest relative or legal guardian. When a patient has been deemed legally incompetent, the health care agency and the physician are obligated to obtain consent from the individual who has been named the legal guardian of that particular patient. This situation exists only when a court order has been obtained stating that, in an appropriate hearing, the person has been deemed legally incompetent, and a legal guardian has been appointed.

In the absence of legal determination of incompetency, however, both the health care agency and the physician are obligated to obtain consent from the nearest relative when it is clear from the assessment that the patient is clinically incompetent. This situation occurs when manifest physical symptoms indicate that the patient cannot consent to treatment—for example, the patient is comatose or unconscious. Then the next of kin may consent to the treatment proposed. In some jurisdictions, a priority for next of kin exists that is the same as that for autopsy. It is suggested that the nurse examine the statutory or case law in the particular jurisdiction to find out what priority exists in that state. Most states have established priority as follows: the surviving spouse is first in line; then adult children, adult grandchildren, parents, brothers and/or sisters, nephews and/or nieces, grandparents, uncles and/or aunts, cousins, and stepchildren, in that order.

A problem may arise for the physician or hospital if consent is requested and the next of kin refuses to comply on religious or other grounds. In this situation, the hospital administrator or physician may consider the possibility of obtaining a court order giving authority to render the needed treatment to the individual who is either incompetent by reason of a medical condition or unable to give consent by reason of being comatose or unconscious. Another problem may arise when several relatives who are on the same level of priority for consent disagree as to the advisability of treatment. Again, the attending physician and hospital administrator should examine the possibility of obtaining a court order permitting the course of action that should be taken.

What is the nurse's role in a situation in which the patient appears incompetent or unable to give consent or authorization for a procedure? If a physician asks a nurse to obtain written authorization or consent for a particular procedure, and, in the course of attempting to do so, the nurse observes that the patient appears incompetent, confused, or unable in some way to consent to the procedure, that nurse has the responsibility of notifying the physician of the apparent state of that patient. She must also document her observations in the nurses' notes along with the information that she has notified the physician of this fact. At that point, the responsibility for obtaining consent or clarifying the patient's competency rests with the treating physician.

Can a person committed to a mental institution or psychiatric unit consent to treatment? Even though it appears the law is changing somewhat in this regard, a person who voluntarily submits to care in a mental health facility retains the right to accept or refuse treatment unless the person is found to be incompetent. However, the current trend in the law is to recognize the right even of those involuntarily committed to decide for or to refuse treatment. A number of cases exist that involve the right of mental institutions to use drugs or neurosurgical procedures to control a patient's violent or antisocial behavior. In view of the varying state laws in regard to this issue, a nurse who works in a mental health facility has an obligation to learn what the institution's policy is regarding treatment to be rendered to both voluntarily and involuntarily committed patients.

Who may give consent for a patient residing in a transitional living situation? The same guidelines are used for patients in transitional living situations as for those who are hospitalized or institutionalized. Therefore, unless adjudicated incompetent, a patient can authorize treatment for himself or herself. If, in the nursing assessment process, it is clinically apparent to the nurse that the patient does not understand what is happening, it is the nurse's duty to notify the physician of this fact. If the physician finds the patient unable to consent, then next-of-kin consent becomes mandatory.

Home health care agencies should provide nurses who work in home settings with guidelines as to correct procedure when the nurse recognizes the need for immediate action in an emergency situation, the patient is incompetent to consent, and no relative is available.

Does a spouse have a right to information given to a patient during the informing process? When a patient is conscious and mentally capable of giving consent for treatment, the consent of the spouse is unnecessary. As stated earlier, when the patient is unconscious or otherwise unable to consent, the spouse is the individual from whom authorization should be sought.

Recently, serious questions have arisen concerning the need for spousal consent for procedures that may in some way affect the marital relationship—for example, abortion or sterilization. In the case of *Planned Parenthood of Central Missouri v. Danforth* [428 U.S. 52, 96 S.Ct. 2831 (1974)], the U.S. Supreme Court, by its ruling, struck down state statutes requiring the consent of the spouse as a precondition to abortion. Obviously, case law in this area is not fully developed and, as a matter of practicality, registered nurses should look to their own state laws and their institutions' policy and procedure for information about how to proceed when marital relationships may be involved.

Is patient consent required for inoculations? Although the administration procedure for various types of inoculations is relatively simple, it is still advisable to obtain the patient's written consent to the inoculation. The consent form should specify the exact type of inoculation to be given, from what substance it is derived, the purpose thereof, and any risks associated with the procedure. Many inoculation programs require the signing of a certain consent form that is drawn up by a specific governmental agency. A nurse working in a health care facility has the responsibility of knowing what forms are required in specific inoculation programs.

Is the patient's signed consent needed when photographs are to be taken of him or her? In the case of educational photographic activity, it is necessary to obtain written consent or permission for the taking of photographs, whether a still camera, motion picture, or any other photographic mechanism is used. The patient's permission is also required for photographing by a newspaper reporter. In the latter case, the physician's permission may also be required. If a private photographer desires to take pictures for another purpose—for example, a future lawsuit—then it is advisable to obtain both the patient's and the physician's permission in writing.

The nurse who works closely with the patient on an ongoing basis should be aware of the employing institution's policy and procedure in this regard as well as the manner in which it is to be implemented. Then, when confronted by an individual desirous of taking pictures, the nurse will know what to document in the medical record before the photographer may proceed.

What special procedural safeguards need to be followed when investigational drugs or experimental procedures are being used on a patient? The federal government has established that any experimental procedure or medication used for patient treatment requires a number of additional informed consent specifications when such treatment is part of a special protocol approved by the institution's review board. It is not within the ambit of this discussion to enumerate all the requirements of such a process. However, the nurse who works in a research environment should be aware of which patients may be placed on a special protocol and what additional informed consent, if any, may be required. The nurse should also be cognizant of the manner in which the institution handles these protocols and how the physician obtains consent for an experimental process.

Under what circumstances does a patient have the right to refuse treatment? Even though most health care professionals understand that a person may have the right to refuse treatment for religious reasons, many are not aware that a legally competent patient of the age of majority has the right to refuse any treatment on the basis of a reason that is of a purely personal nature. However, in a refusal-of-treatment situation, especially when such refusal is honored and death or serious harm to the patient results, questions arise as to the clinical competency of the patient at the time of the refusal. For example, a person who refuses treatment may be highly sedated, hysterical, traumatized in some way, or unable to understand effectively the total ramifications of refusal of treatment. Therefore, when refusal would result in either death or serious harm to the patient, it is advisable for the nurse to notify the doctor and for a thorough evaluation to be made by the attending physician, as well as by a consulting physician, to determine the clinical competency of the patient to make judgments at the time of the refusal.

If the patient is deemed incompetent to do this, it would be appropriate for the hospital administrator or the physician, or both acting jointly, to attempt to obtain a court order to perform the procedure. When the competency of the patient is not questioned, a simple refusal of treatment form, along with a release of responsibility form, must be signed by the patient who refuses the treatment. Such forms are available in most health care institutions.

Does the hospital or institutional release form protect the nurse from liability when a patient or the patient's family refuses treatment? Most institutions require that a release form be completed by the patient or by someone legally authorized to act for the patient who refuses some advised treatment. This release acts as evidence that the patient understands and voluntarily assumes any risks incident to the refusal of treatment. Usually this form will later protect the hospital, the employees, and the physician if the patient asserts that proper care was not given. Of course, the question of the competency of the patient immediately prior to and during the refusal and execution of the release form becomes paramount. Therefore, it is essential for both the nurses' notes and the physician's notes to contain very detailed documentation describing the outward signs that indicate the rationality and competency of the patient at the time of refusal and of signing the release.

2
Standards of Care

Introduction

A standard may be viewed as a model established by a recognized authority. It is a level or degree of quality considered adequate for a specific purpose. Standards define what should be done and identify conditions under which one can reasonably expect quality care to be given (Alexander, 1978, p. 71). Nurses have long been involved with care standards of various types.

Types of Standards of Nursing Care

Nursing Licensure Board and Legislative Standards

The legal standards for nursing education and the legal practice of nursing are the province of the Nursing Licensure Board and the legislative bodies of each state. Thus, for the most part, nurses are familiar with the statute that defines the practice of professional nursing in the state in which they are licensed to practice. They are not always familiar with the regulations regarding nursing practice that are promulgated in their respective states and how these differ from the licensure statute. However, it is imperative for the professional nurse to be aware of these differences.

In most states the statute is very broadly worded, and the scope of nursing is very carefully defined. This definition is both necessary and helpful, but it is only a starting point for establishing effective guidelines as to specific nursing functions.

To discover how a licensing body in a given state looks at a specific function, it is necessary to examine carefully the regulations promulgated pursuant to the statute. It is these regulations that inform nurses about the proper delegation of responsibility for specific tasks, the type of training or instruction required to perform the tasks, and whether it is necessary for the physician to write an order for certain procedures before the nurse undertakes to perform these procedures. Thus, it can be seen that the regulations are particularly helpful in delineating accountability for many of the specific functions of nursing within a given state.

Joint Statements

The joint statement is one type of standard. Such statements have been drawn up by the nursing, medical, pharmaceutical, and dental bodies in many states. They are expressions of mutually agreed upon positions about critical issues that impact upon the practice of more than one health care discipline. They may be referred to for information about how a specific concern has been resolved by either the licensing body or a group of professional associations representing various health care professionals.

Institutional Policies and Procedures

Institutional policies and procedures give the nurse additional insight into the standards of practice for which he or she is held accountable. Many nurses understand that externally imposed criteria can be used to delineate a legal standard of care. However, internally imposed standards set forth in institutional or departmental policies and procedures indicate what standard of care exists for a particular institution or agency, above and beyond that imposed by external bodies. Consequently, these policies and procedures must be drawn up in such a fashion that they can be applied in an integrated, multidisciplinary health care setting and

Standards of Care

so that the staff understands what is intended by each particular policy and procedure.

It must be borne in mind that the standards imposed by the Nursing Licensure Board and the state laws are minimal in nature. Therefore, even though a health care institution or individual has lived up to the written standards, it is possible for a jury or court of law to find that a professional has not lived up to a standard of "reasonableness" imposed by a jury or by arbitrators after they have heard evidence and testimony presented by both sides in a legal action. So it is important for the registered nurse to keep abreast of developments and trends in case law affecting the practice of nursing. It is strongly advised that every orientation program for new employees include a session on these nursing standards as well as information regarding where the nurse may obtain copies of the standards.

Accrediting Agency Standards

Many other health care organizations are involved with standards that ultimately affect nursing standards. In 1963 the Board of Trustees of the American Hospital Association (AHA) established regulations for the acceptance of hospitals for registration via an accreditation process. The accreditation survey is conducted by the Joint Commission on the Accreditation of Hospitals (JCAH). Today the standards of the JCAH are varied and complex, and nurses need to be knowledgeable about current standards, recommendations, and interpretations set forth by the commission.

One of the most recent standards to have broad implications for all health disciplines is the 1981 JCAH "Standards of Quality Assurance." The principle identified in this statement is as follows:

> The hospital shall demonstrate a consistent endeavor to deliver patient care that is optimal within available resources and consistent with achievable goals. A major component in the application of this principle is the operation of a quality assurance program.

The standard states that:

> There shall be evidence of a well-defined organized program designed to enhance patient care through the ongoing objective assessment of important aspects of patient care and the correction of identified problems. [JCAH, 1981, p. 151]

Analysis of this statement makes it clear that it is the responsibility of the governing body to establish, maintain, and support, through the hospital administration and medical staff, an ongoing quality assurance program that includes effective mechanisms for reviewing and evaluating patient care (as well as an appropriate response to findings). Further, it is stated in "Standards of Quality Assurance" that to obtain maximal benefit, any approach to quality assurance must focus on the resolution of known or suspected problems that impact directly or indirectly on patients or, when indicated, on areas with potential for substantial improvement in patient care. It is incumbent on a hospital to document evidence of an effective quality assurance program.

For a quality assurance program to be fully effective, it must use objective criteria to assess and evaluate the quality of patient care in such a way that identified problems will be corrected. Each discipline and department in an institution must carry on the assurance activity and monitor its results through an auditing procedure. Therefore, it is incumbent on nurses to become involved in an integrated, coordinated approach to quality assurance by an evaluation of their own functions in relation to the totality of patient care given within a particular institution.

In the JCAH "Standard," reference is made to the various kinds of criteria that can be used to assess problems. One criterion specifically mentioned is the standard of practice of professional organizations. In the case of nursing, the American Nurses' Association standards of practice discussed earlier are applicable. The very fact that the JCAH alludes to such standards as appropriate assessment criteria makes it imperative that the professional nurse be knowledgeable about their substance and content (JCAH, 1981, p. 152).

The standards established by the American Hospital Association in 1965 identified six essential elements of optimum health services that have implications for professional nurses:

1. A team approach to the care of the individual, in which the health professions providing services are integrated and coordinated under the leadership of the physician.
2. A spectrum of services that includes specific treatment, rehabilitation, education, and prevention.
3. A coordinated community and/or regional system that incorporates the full spectrum of health services and provides for coordination of care from the time of the patient's primary contact with the system through the community hospital to the university hospital and/or medical center and other health agencies. Each should provide the portion of the total spectrum of health services that is feasible in terms of the type of community it serves and the overall pattern of health facilities of the region in which it exists.
4. Continuity among the hospital aspects of patient care, the community, the physician, and the health agencies rendering particular services.
5. Organizations of the hospital care of both ambulatory and bed patients into a continuum with common or integrated services.
6. Continuing programs of evaluation and research in the quality of services provided and in their adequacy in meeting needs of the patient and community. [Alexander, 1978, pp. 67–68]

A few years later the AHA developed a statement that dealt with the minimum expectations of a registered nurse. In essence, this statement is akin to a standard of practice statement because it defines the role of clinical judgment and the assessment function. It looks at the function of communication and coordination in meeting patient needs through the team approach. It also discusses the functions of supervisors as teachers and directors of those individuals who provide nursing care through the following:

1. Planning of nursing care pursuant to the medical care plan of the physician. Assessment of patient needs for nursing and establishment of objectives for nursing actions on a continuing basis.
2. Implementing plans of nursing care in accordance with objectives of the nursing care plan and organization, direction, and supervision of nursing personnel in giving nursing care. In the assignment of nursing personnel, registered nurses give care to patients whose condition requires their professional competence and skills.
3. Evaluating the quality of nursing care in terms of the extent to which objectives of the nursing plan are met. Appraisal of the quality of nursing care, the performance of nursing personnel, and the proper use of equipment and supplies in rendering nursing care.
4. Coordinating patient care activities. By virtue of the strategic position the registered nurse occupies as the most constant figure relating and communicating both with the patient and with members of the professional staff in providing patient services, he or she can coordinate activities to achieve to the greatest extent possible a unified approach to the care of the patient.
5. Teaching to nursing personnel the nursing care of patients in relation to the objectives of the nursing care plan. Determination of specific nursing knowledge and skills that need to be learned by nursing personnel. [Alexander, 1978, p. 69]

The ANA has also promulgated standards of practice over the years. In 1965 the ANA published its first *Standards for Organizing Nursing Services*. At the ANA biennial convention in May, 1974, the first priority for the next biennium was defined as the improvement of nursing practice through the implementation of the ANA standards of practice. The ANA has continued to develop and disseminate standards of practice in several clinical areas. These standards provide a model for guiding the development of a reliable means of assessing the quality of the nursing process.

Nurses who are not familiar with the specific standards that apply to their clinical interests should obtain a copy of these standards from the ANA because the standards can be used as evidence in malpractice proceedings to prove that a standard of care was or was not met.

Standards of Care

Standards of practice have been the subject of increasing governmental attention since the early 1970s. In 1972 the U.S. Congress passed the Social Security Amendment that provided for the establishment of the Professional Standards Review Organization (PSRO),* consisting of physicians who were given the overall responsibility for ongoing review and evaluation of health care services that are covered by Medicare, Medicaid, and Maternal Child Health Programs. Although physicians were given the primary responsibility, the manual also indicated that PSROs would be expected to show that nonphysician health care personnel must develop and modify criteria and standards for their individual areas of practice.

Safety Standards

The JCAH has established minimum safety standards for a physical environment that is safe for patients, visitors, and staff who work in health care institutions. In addition, in 1970 the Occupational Safety and Health Act (OSHA) was passed. It is the authors' feeling that even though OSHA is currently under attack, its operations will continue in a streamlined fashion. The Department of Labor is entrusted with the enforcement of OSHA standards.

Many nurses do not know about these various safety standards. While they are minimal, not optimal, and not all directly related to nursing care, a professional nurse needs to know how various aspects of these standards apply to his or her specific job responsibilities. An explanation of these safety standards should be an essential part of any dynamic orientation program for new staff members.

Nurses need to know how these standards are used in court cases. Nurses also need to know what standard to use when confronted with two standards, one of which may appear to impose an

---

*At the time of writing, the PSRO is still in existence; it probably will be phased out by the Reagan administration. It is impossible to say when or if some other agency will be substituted for it or assigned its work.

inconsistent or greater burden on him or her within the health care setting.

Interprofessional issues arise when it appears that a specific standard of nursing practice is not being followed because of conflicts or inconsistencies between the job descriptions among health care professionals working in the system.

The appendixes to this chapter contain samples of a nurse practice act, practice regulations, and joint statements, all from the state of Pennsylvania. All professional nurses should be familiar with comparable documents governing the practice of nursing in their particular states and should have their own personal copies or, at a minimum, ready access to them.

Questions and Answers

Where does the nurse go to find out what standards are applicable to specific practice situations? Although many nurses interviewed by the authors were aware of and had read the professional nursing law in the states where they work, many were not aware that the law is merely a starting point for development of standards of practice, especially for specific practice situations. First, the nurse must read and understand the meaning behind each word in the professional nursing law of the specific jurisdiction of his or her employment. Usually, one of the sections in the statute will allow the professional licensing board of that state the power and authority to promulgate new regulations that deal with specific areas of nursing practice. For example, regulations may deal with the administration of medications, resuscitation, or defibrillation.

To find out exactly what the parameters are for specific nursing tasks, the nurse must go to the nursing regulations after having read the nursing law. Usually, the regulations will identify the parameters under which the nurse must work. For example, they will tell him or her whether special education is needed to carry out a particular task and whether specific tasks have to be ordered by a

Standards of Care

physician in writing. One must also read the regulations carefully to determine whether certain items in the regulations are mandatory or permissive in nature. Usually, the professional licensing board that prepares the regulations will use the words "must" or "shall" when a regulation is mandatory. If the nursing law and the regulation do not provide guidance for specific nursing tasks, the next source to check is the nurse's own institutional or departmental policies and procedures. Most institutions develop policy and procedures for special tasks not covered by the law or the regulations. Sometimes an institutional policy or procedure will require duties in connection with a specific task that are above and beyond those required by the statute and the state licensure body. Thus, the nurse must know and abide by the institutional policy and procedure.

In addition, it is important to read one's particular state law and regulations to see whether the licensing board in that state has incorporated the professional nursing code of ethics or professional association rules as criteria for safe and effective practice. In Pennsylvania, a specific regulation states that guidelines promulgated by professional associations and the accrediting bodies will be criteria for effective and safe nursing practice [(49 Pa. Code 321.11(d)].

We must also look to those standards promulgated by all professional associations, such as ANA, and to accrediting bodies to find out what specific elements are included in defining effective and current nursing practice. The JCAH rules will also apply to those who work in a hospital. All these sources can be used to decide which standards to use in specific nursing situations. Usually, one of those sources will furnish guidance as to specific nursing tasks. Keep in mind that expert opinion as provided in textbooks, journals, or by expert witnesses may also be used to define the standard for a specific nursing practice situation. In addition, a judge and jury may find specific nursing tasks to be reasonably or unreasonably carried out, despite complete compliance with all the applicable standards. This may seem confusing, but if we keep in mind that all the legislative standards are minimal in nature, it will be less difficult to realize that a higher standard of care may be imposed upon the nurse, or that the jury may find the conduct to be unreasonable even though all the *minimal* standards were met. *How much weight is given to standards promulgated by various accrediting bodies and professional associations?* This question is often asked by registered nurses at various levels who are confused as to the nature of these standards in relation to state statutes, regulations, and common law. It should be noted that state statutory and regulatory standards are a primary source of law to indicate what the standard of practice is for a specific nursing task. However, standards and codes of conduct promulgated by various accrediting bodies and professional associations have been held to be evidence of a standard of practice in the industry itself.

The decision of *Darling v. Charleston Community Memorial Hospital* and its progeny have held that standards promulgated by the various accrediting agencies, such as those imposed by JCAH, are evidence of a minimal standard of care for that particular task [33 Il.2d 326, 211 N.E.2d 253 (1965) *cert. denied,* 383 U.S. 946 (1966)]. The *Darling* decision concerned an 18-year-old boy who was brought to the emergency room for treatment of a fractured leg. The cast applied by the emergency room physician was too tight and lacked sufficient padding. Many times the plaintiff complained of discomfort to the nursing staff and emergency room physician. His toes were swollen, discolored, and lacked sensation. Despite his complaints, the cast was left on for four days. The nurses knew the symptoms and signs of gangrene, but no report of this was made to the medical staff; or, if it was, no action was taken. An orthopedic surgeon was not consulted. The patient eventually lost his leg, and the hospital emergency room doctor and the nursing staff were held responsible.

In this case, a statewide regulation and an internal policy of the institution both required that, in such a situation, the emergency room physician is required to secure consultation by an orthopedic surgeon. This was not done. Additionally, the court held that the health regulation and the internal policy and procedure that related to the consultation by the surgeon created a standard of practice for that institution. The hospital breached its standard of care since it did not obtain a consultation.

There was also an issue of inadequate staffing in the emergency department, according to the JCAH requirements. In this regard, too, the court held that the JCAH accrediting rule became the minimal standard of practice for the nursing staff in the emergency department. The nursing and supervisory personnel of the hospital were held responsible on two other bases:

1. for failing to monitor the patient's condition adequately and
2. for failing to have a recording system available so that nursing knowledge could be applied for the benefit of the patient in the case.

Thus, it can be seen that standards of practice promulgated by various agencies, in conjunction with standards promulgated by the state statutes and regulations, common law, and internal policies and procedures, can act as evidence of a standard of care throughout the health care industry. When a complicated situation arises, all these standards must be examined in an integrated, coordinated way so that each one may be viewed as possible independent evidence of the standard of care for the institution or the health care professional involved.

What elements are necessary to prove a negligence or professional liability case against a health care professional? Many nurses in seminars conducted by the authors think that any error in treatment or nursing practice or any injury to a patient could give rise to a liability situation. Of course, questions of liability arise whenever an error is committed or whenever a patient is unexpectedly injured. However, a number of points must be proven by the patient before a tentative claim becomes an actual liability case. In most situations, the plaintiff's attorney must prove four things:

1. that a standard of case existed in the given situation,
2. that the standard of care was breached or broken,
3. the proximate causation, and
4. damage.

Generally, it must be remembered that, as with malpractice involving physicians, the relevant standard of care must be identified in such a way as to bring up the question of what a reasonably prudent nurse engaged in the same or similar practice would do in the same situation. A developing line or tort law has stated that the health care professional must not subject a patient to an unreasonable risk of harm. The question that has to be answered is what constitutes an unreasonable risk of harm. A nurse may subject a patient to unreasonable risk through lack of knowledge or failure to recognize the inherent danger of a situation. The various sources of law may provide the practitioner with a guideline as to what constitutes reasonable nursing action so that a patient need not be subjected to an unreasonable risk to his or her health.

As to breach of the standard of care, this may be proven in a courtroom in several ways. For example, it may be proven through review of the medical record by the plaintiff's attorney to ascertain whether certain nursing tasks were not documented and perhaps were not done. Sometimes nursing personnel are called to testify in the patient's behalf to point out that perhaps the nursing personnel did not know the institutional policy and procedures for specific situations. Breach may also be proven by the patient. Usually, a number of techniques is used, but it is the medical record that becomes all important. In the usual case, documentation is scanty and, since memory fades with time, nursing personnel often cannot remember what was done on a specific date three or four years after the occurrence of an incident. Because of its importance in court cases, documentation is discussed in depth in Chapter 3.

In order to prove proximate causation, the plaintiff's attorney must find a causal link between breach of the applicable standard of care and the damage or injury to the patient. Causation is often difficult to prove. It is not often that a single individual in a health care setting can be said to be the only one who brought about a particular harm to a particular patient. Complex relationships between health care professionals frequently lead to the assumption of multiple causation when injury occurs. The legal system has devised a number of tests to identify the causation element. One frequently used today is the "substantial factor" test: if harm should come to a patient, it is only necessary for the plaintiff's attorney, in order to impose legal responsibility, to prove that a particular health care professional's negligent conduct was a substantial factor contributing to that harm. It need not be the full causative agent, and it may not even be the principal cause. For that health care professional to be held legally responsible, it is sufficient that his or her conduct contributed substantially to the harm that occurred to the plaintiff. Others who could also be held liable include the hospital and other physicians or nurses who were involved in caring for the patient.

Damage, the fourth element that must be proven, consists of a number of items. In the professional liability situation, physical harm to the patient must be shown before a liability situation arises. "Pain and suffering," in and of themselves, are not sufficient to prove damage; physical harm to the patient must be proven. Other items that may be included in the damage category are expenses incurred for hospitalization, physician bills—whether in the past or in the future—loss of earning capacity, and loss of support and comfort.

Does it ever happen in health care settings that the four specific elements of a negligence need not be proven? In the area of negligence, the legal doctrine of *res ipsa loquitur,* a Latin term meaning "the thing speaks for itself," describes a situation in which causation need not be proven. In such instances, the harm is so apparent that even a lay person can readily perceive that such harm would not or could not occur without negligence. When *res ipsa loquitur* is used as the theory of liability, the plaintiff need only prove:

1. that the event was such that it would not have occurred in the absence of negligence,
2. that the instrumentality or agency causing the event was in exclusive control of the defendant(s),
3. that the event was not due to any conduct—in other words, contributory negligence—on the part of the patient.

Nurses must differentiate the doctrine of *res ipsa loquitur* from strict liability when liability without negligence may be found. Strict liability is usually found in situations involving product defect and failure, whereas *res ipsa loquitur* usually occurs when mechanical instruments have been used, when a surgical instrument has been left in the body, or when surgery has been done on the wrong part of the body. In the famous case of *Ybarra v. Spangard*, the patient, in the course of undergoing an appendectomy, sustained traumatic injuries to a formerly healthy shoulder [25 Ca.2d 4868, 154 P.2d 678 (1944)]. At the trial, the patient testified that he was pulled onto the operating table and his back was placed against two hard objects that were positioned at the top of his shoulders. Because he was anesthetized, he did not know what was going on. Upon awakening from the anesthetic, he complained of a sharp pain in his shoulder. Eventually, paralysis and atrophy of the muscles around the shoulder developed.

In his lawsuit, Mr. Ybarra named all the physicians and nurses who were involved in the surgical procedure and in his postoperative care. In the case, the court determined that even though the patient could not obtain direct proof of negligence, the doctrine of *res ipsa loquitur* placed the defendants in a position to explain why the injury occurred. Ultimately, the defendants were held liable for the patient's resultant injuries.

From a practical standpoint, the evolution of this doctrine in the United States has resulted in a tremendous number of documentation requirements in several departments within health care institutions. For example, operating room personnel are now required to count every instrument, sponge, or other foreign object that was used in the operation before first closure and second closure and to document the count. This requirement evolved only after the theory *res ipsa loquitur* developed. It must be remembered that, in theory, this doctrine involves not only the law but also evidence in a court of law and, therefore, is of significant concern to attorneys.

What is the relationship between standards of nursing practice and legal standards of care? A standard of nursing practice is merely one indicator of what constitutes a legal standard of care in a specific situation. As stated earlier, the nursing standards, whether they be gleaned from regulations, institutional policies and procedures, or accrediting body rules, must be looked upon as minimal in nature; and even though all of these are followed, a court of law or a jury may impose a higher legal standard. For example, a jury may, on the basis of facts brought before it, decide that a nurse did not act as a reasonably prudent nurse would have acted in utilizing the knowledge and skills of the profession even though the nurse on trial did meet the specific nursing standard of practice for a particular procedure. As confusing as it might seem, the court may hold a nurse accountable for an even higher degree of reasonableness than called for by the standard if, within the facts brought to the court's attention, a reasonable nurse should have acted differently in a specific circumstance.

For this reason, courts have stated that the standards of practice are the guidelines or evidence of the legal standard of care in a specific situation. Consequently, the legal standard of care is only one element that must be proven in a total liability case. A nurse may be guilty of the most flagrant unprofessional conduct in the course of his or her practice, may violate dozens of nursing standards, and yet not be subject to legal liability if no injury or damage occurred to a patient.

Does an institution-wide or a departmental policy and procedure regulation create a standard of practice or a legal standard of care? Many health care professionals do not realize that when policies and procedures, or protocols, are set forth in a manual or written form for the staff, a standard of practice is being created for that particular institution or department. In effect, these internal guidelines create an additional standard of care for the health professional than those imposed externally. Such policies and procedures are discoverable and may be admitted into evidence to show what the standard of practice or care is in a given institution.

The nursing policy and procedure manual is usually the first place a plaintiff's attorney looks when investigating a professional liability case that involves the nursing staff; he or she needs to find out whether the nursing staff complied with its own standards of care. Therefore, it is highly important to educate nursing staff members as to the importance of their being aware of current policies and procedures and of correct documentation regarding adherence to these policies and procedures during a patient's hospital stay. It is also important for nurses to remember, when they sit on a policy and procedures committee, that they must establish rules and regulations that are both practical and enforceable. Policies and procedures should not be written merely to satisfy some externally imposed standard.

In a court of law, are nurses held to national standards or to community standards of practice? This is a question often posed by nurses, and rightfully so, for the standards to which a nurse is currently held, whether they be community or national standards, are still in the developmental stage.

The first thing to remember is that a registered nurse is held to a prevailing standard of care that requires a level of performance of competent nursing in like or similar situations. As case law has developed, nurses have been held to a standard of practice in a like or similar community. In the case of *Hiatt v. Groce* [523 P.2d 320 (Kans. 1974)], the court stated that expert testimony must be presented by a member of the same profession to show a standard of practice in a same or similar community and under the same or similar circumstances. However, nurses who hold themselves out as specialists, such as nurse anesthetists, operating room nurses, or intensive care nurses, have been held to standards of care and skill exercised by those in the same specialty as delineated by a national standard. The reason for this is that nurses working in such specialty areas should be held to a standard set by more sophisticated or competitive institutions, such as those found in an urban or university setting, since in these settings the care required in specialty situations is more defined, more clearly delineated, and more technologically oriented than in other settings.

How is "reasonable nursing practice" determined by a court of law? The patient usually has the burden of proof to show the court and the jury that he or she has a valid case of negligence, whether it be against a health care professional, a hospital, a medical staff member, or a professional nurse. To do this, every party to the case—the patient, hospital representative, and health care professional—will have an opportunity to testify and to present evidence as to why a standard of care was or was not met. Counsel for each side will bring to the court's or the jury's attention the law, regulations, institutional policies and procedures, factual testimony, medical record documentation or the lack thereof, and expert opinion about the adequacy or inadequacy of care that was provided to the patient.

The initial question to which the judge will respond is whether the patient has presented sufficient evidence to bring the case before the jury's attention. If it is decided that the patient's attorney has a *prima facie* (a Latin term meaning "at first view") case of negligence or proof that the four elements of negligence have been met, the judge will then allow the defendant parties— the health care professionals—to place their evidence into the case. Because the courts have held that the standards imposed by external bodies are minimal in nature, even if all standards have been met, the jury may still question whether the health care provider acted reasonably in the situation. In such an instance, the credibility of the witnesses, the evidence as presented in medical records, and the expert opinion will be weighed by the jury. The jury must then determine whether the health care provider acted reasonably and whether the evidence as presented by the patient is reasonable.

In some cases, the courts have gone so far as to impose a duty of affirmative action on the part of the nurse. The case of *Goff v. Doctor's General Hospital* was concerned with a patient who died after a hemorrage following the delivery of a baby [166 Cal.App.2d 314, 333 P.2d 25 (1958)]. The physician had made an incision into the cervix to relieve a constricting band of muscles. The hospital policy stated that blood could be administered by a nurse only upon a physician's written order. In holding for the patient, the court emphasized that the nurse knew of the peril to the mother and knew the cause and origin of the peril. Her inaction, even though in compliance with hospital policy and procedure and with physician orders, was sufficient to show negligent conduct on the part of the nurse independently of the physician—she failed to act to obtain help for a mother who was bleeding to death. The jury and the court held that the duty of affirmative action on the nurse's part extended beyond the written standards. Therefore, it is possible for a jury to find that a health care professional's action or inaction was unreasonable even though the written policies and procedures and the externally imposed standards were all met.

What documents can be used in a law suit to determine whether a standard of practice for the care afforded to a patient had been met? As to the standards of nursing practice, all the externally imposed standards, such as the laws of a certain state, regulations, codes of conduct, accrediting body rules, and professional association rules, may be placed into evidence to show a standard of practice. Of course, a health care professional's attorney may argue that the rules are either applicable or inapplicable. However, the point to be made is that the health care professional should know to which bodies and which rules he or she is accountable. Nursing practice standards as stated in textbooks may be admitted into evidence in cases; however, they are also subject to dispute and may be refuted or attacked by use of other textbooks that present a different view. Further, institutional or departmental policies may be used to indicate the standard of practice. Again, those policies and procedures may be subject to questioning by the defense counsel in the case.

With regard to the care afforded a patient, the medical record is probably the most important document to show either a lack of care or to describe the type of care given to a patient. Many persons who work in health care institutions do not realize what goes into the official medical record of the institution. The nurse needs to know whether the nurses' notes are made a part of the official medical record in a particular place of employment. Although some hospitals destroy them, we strongly recommend that nurses' notes be preserved intact. For example, x-rays, fetal monitor strips, consent forms, and EKG readings are usually made part of the official medical record; if not, it is advisable that they be retained as an official record. Certain items, such as a Kardex file or records of scheduling patterns, may not become part of the medical record. However, these items should be preserved by the nursing department to show that staffing was adequate in a particular unit on a particular day. Such documentation may be of immense interest to the defense in a professional liability suit against a health care professional. The Kardex can be used as a source of information if the patient is ever readmitted.

How does the nurse know if he or she is acting in accordance with standards of nursing care when he or she works on a team with other health care professionals? All health care providers licensed to practice should look at the practice act within their particular states to find out what constitutes permissive and mandatory practice for their particular disciplines. Usually, the law will be very broadly written so that changes do not have to be made continually in the law itself. However, the usual practice is to give the licensing boards within the states the power and authority to promulgate rules and regulations regarding specific practice acts in what is known as "the enabling legislation" in the act. Hence, most of the practice acts will also have concurrent regulations that delineate the scope of the practice in certain concrete situations. For example, in the nursing practice act, the rules and regulations may apply to the administration of medications, the administration of IVs and intravenous medications, defibrillation, monitoring devices, and the administration of anesthesia. The rules and regulations will specify how and when these tasks may be performed by registered nurses or to whom they may be delegated. It is very important that nurses read these rules and regulations carefully so as to know the conditions under which they may perform certain nursing functions.

In addition, the job description or policy and procedures statement provided by the institution will delineate what is permissible nursing practice or scope of practice within a particular institution. For example, a particular nursing function described in the practice act may be inconsistent with the direction of the institution and the institution will decide that a more limited job description is in order. Therefore, the nurse must go to all these sources to determine the proper scope of nursing practice in his or her particular place of employment.

Questions may also arise as to the role of nursing in regard to other health care professionals, such as physician assistants or physicians themselves. These questions may be answered in the practice act. Usually, it is imperative to look at the relationship between the nursing practice act, regulations, and job descriptions and the practice act governing the other health care professionals, such as physicians. However, if a nurse is faced with a particularly sensitive issue, the problem should not be solved on an individual basis within the institution; instead, it should be approached on an interdisciplinary basis in order to determine what is correct practice for that particular institution.

What are the most effective ways of dealing with conflicting or inconsistent care standards among various health care professionals? Health care professionals need to realize that there may be serious inconsistencies among the many standards set up for various categories of health care workers. Proper integration and coordination of standards within a particular health care setting are vital to quality care. It is probably within the best interest of all parties concerned for each discipline to look first at the mandatory and permissive functions allowed them within their own practice acts and laws.

Second, the various disciplines must attempt to integrate any inconsistent standards into a workable system within the institution. When a problem arises that concerns pharmacists, nurses, and doctors, all three of these professional groups should sit on the multidisciplinary committee that is appointed to resolve the problem.

Sometimes problems are taken to an external agency that has authority over both licensing bodies. For example, in many states, issues have arisen concerning the conflicting nature of the licensing and practice act for physician assistants and nurses. The licensing bodies of those groups have taken the questioned sections of the laws and regulations to the State Attorney General's Office for an opinion and resolution of the problem. When such an opinion was unsatisfactory to the parties, they could then consider judicial avenues. For example, in the states of Iowa, Washington, and Michigan, it has been held that the physician assistant acts as an agent of the physician and the nurse should follow the physician assistant's orders as if they were those of a physician [Iowa Atty Gen. Opinion No. 78-12-41 Dec. 30, 1978; Washington State Nurses' Association v. The Board of Medical Examiners, Wash. Sup. Ct. Opinion 46148 (1980); Michigan Atty Gen. Opinion No. 5220, August 31, 1977].

How does a nurse know whether a specific nursing task is mandatory or permissive in nature? The professional nursing law within one's own state holds the answer to this question. In statutory language, the words "must" and "shall" usually denote a mandatory function. A permissive function is denoted by the words "may" and "should." Many times, however, such language is not used in the statute, and the functions of nursing are merely stated in the definition of what constitutes nursing. When this is the case, it is necessary to look to the regulations to discern whether the language in the regulations is mandatory or permissive in nature. Often the language does not include either "must" or "shall." Then it may be necessary to depend on the interpretive power of the state licensing board for clarification on this point. The licensing board in a particular state may have discretionary rule-making or interpretive power, and will look at the legislative history of the act for information regarding whether a specific nursing function should be deemed mandatory or permissive.

How can a nurse determine what constitutes proper nursing practice when a specific nursing function is not addressed in a state of nursing practice act? It may be important to find out whether the regulations under the act incorporate or make reference to the standards or guidelines espoused by various professional associations or accrediting bodies. Some state acts incorporate such guidelines and standards as criteria for assuring safe and effective practice. The nurse in a particular state may also look into national or professional association rules or guidelines to discern their recommendations for handling specific nursing practice situations. Sometimes, however, this is an unproductive exercise. In such a case, it may be necessary to obtain an opinion from the licensing board of the particular state. The practice act itself will state whether the board has such interpretive and rule-making power; this varies from state to state. Boards often work together to attempt to derive a resolution to a particular issue that poses problems for various health care professionals in a particular state.

Are there specific standards of practice for the various nursing specialties, and can these guidelines be used in court to support a legal standard of care? Even though the practice of specialty nursing is still evolving, several professional associations have espoused certain guidelines for certain nursing specialties. For example, the ANA has several sets of guidelines available for nurses

Standards of Care

in such specialties as community health nursing, geriatric nursing, and critical care nursing, among others. These guidelines may be used in court to indicate evidence of a standard. But again, determining whether such guidelines constitute the minimal standard depends on whether the guidelines are incorporated in the practice act of the various states, whether they are worded in mandatory or permissive terms, and whether they are intended merely to be recommendations or to be strict rules. In several cases, it has been decided that nurse specialists should be held to the standard of care exercised by those who practice in that specialty across the nation [Webb v. Jorns, supra]. For some nursing specialists, such as nurse practitioners, there is a separate law or set of regulations to govern their behavior; it may be used as evidence to show what the scope of practice and the standard of care are for that particular nursing specialty.

How long after an incident has occurred can a patient bring a case against a health care professional? Every state has a different statute of limitations for various types of cases. Sometimes a case based on general or personal injury has a longer statute of limitations than does a professional liability suit (i.e., a malpractice suit). Some states have established the same statutory period for both types of action. For example, in Pennsylvania a two-year statute of limitations applies to both general liability and professional liability actions.

Another question arises when a nurse is held to be a "health care provider" within a state for purposes of applying the professional liability statute instead of the general liability statute of limitations. Generally, the nurse is held not to be a provider for purposes of applying the shorter malpractice statute of limitations. However, it would be advisable for the nurse to consult an attorney in his or her own state to find out which statute of limitations period is applicable for any possible action against him or her. It is also advisable to ascertain whether a statute will begin to run at the time an incident occurs or at the time the harm or injury is discovered. Some statutes of limitation provide that the patient may bring an action within a specific period of time following the date of the incident or injury, others from the date of the discovery of the incident or injury, whichever is later.

These are the reasons why it is important for the nurse to realize that since the various states differ on this issue, the nurse must be knowledgeable about the state statute that is applicable in his or her jurisdiction.

Do standards of practice allow a nurse or other health care professional to carry out a physician's verbal or telephone order? The staff nurse and the nurse responsible for policy and procedure in an institution must look to the state rules and regulations to find out the department of health or other appropriate body in a particular jurisdiction that has issued guidelines on the carrying out of telephone or verbal orders by a registered nurse. In addition, the nurse should look to the hospital policy and procedure manual and to the medical staff by-laws to ascertain the conditions under which verbal or telephone orders may be taken. Most institutions allow this to be done only in urgent situations and only by certain individuals, such as another physician, a registered nurse, or a licensed practical nurse. Usually, a telephone or verbal order must be documented as such, with a date, the time received, and the full signature of the person taking the order. In most circumstances, state regulations and/or hospital policy and procedure require a countersignature by the prescribing physician within 24 hours after the verbal or telephone order.

What is the role of the registered nurse in the implementation of the 1981 JCAH Statement on Quality Assurance? Under this statement, the institution, as an entity, is responsible for demonstrating and implementing a well-defined, organized program to enhance patient care. The program in the nursing service department would be only one aspect of that entire program, and this department's activities in relation to quality assurance must be integrated into the total plan. According to the standard for nursing administration, it is the responsibility of the nursing department to assure that review and evaluation of the quality and appropriateness of nursing care is accomplished. The individual staff members are obligated to participate in the review. Institutions may achieve implementation of this standard in different ways; however, many are currently achieving this goal through the use of nursing audit committees that evaluate and examine particular problems within the nursing units. A mechanism should be provided to assure that the findings of these committees are disseminated within the nursing departments and to other appropriate departments. If the role of the individual nurse has not been defined in the quality assurance program, nurses in that institution should request that such definition be made part of the quality assurance plan for the nursing service department.

In light of the 1981 Quality Assurance Standards, as promulgated by the JCAH, what steps should the nurse take to guarantee that staffing will be adequate to meet the nursing needs of the patients? Because nurse staffing has been pinpointed as a sensitive issue throughout the country, the persons in charge of carrying out a quality assurance program for a nursing department could undertake a study to determine whether nurse staffing is adequate. Such a study would include the identification of the number of nurses required to staff appropriately the specific units and also the manner in which optimal patient care may be delivered by utilizing available resources. It must be remembered that the "Quality Assurance Standard" promulgated by the JCAH requires only that available resources be used. Therefore, it remains a question whether the institution and nursing administration would meet the quality standard by showing that available resources are being utilized to their fullest potential. We mention it here because the implementation of the JCAH standards is still in the rudimentary stage at this time.

3
Recordkeeping

Introduction

One of a nurse's major responsibilities is to keep clear and accurate medical records, the primary functions of which are:

1. to assist in planning patient care and in evaluating the patient's condition and ongoing treatment;
2. to document the course of the patient's medical evaluation, treatment, and change in condition;
3. to document communication between the responsible practitioner and any other health professionals contributing to the patient's care;
4. to assist in protecting the legal interest of the patient, the hospital, and the responsible practitioner; and
5. to provide data for use in continuing education and research (JCAH, 1981, p. 83).

The *Standards of Nursing Practice* of the ANA stresses the importance of recordkeeping so that "the collection of data about the health status of the client or patient is systematic and continuous. Data are accessible, communicated and recorded." This implies that documentation of the medical record must include the nursing care plan and its mode of implementation (ANA, 1973).

Another standard that emphasizes the role of documentation is the following:

> The nursing process (assessment, planning, intervention, evaluation) shall be documented for each hospitalized patient from admission through discharge. Each patient's nursing needs shall be assessed by a registered nurse at the time of admission or within the period established by nursing department/service policy. These assessment data shall be consistent with the medical plan of care and shall be available to all nursing personnel involved in the care of the patient.
>
> A registered nurse must plan each patient's nursing care and, whenever possible, nursing goals should be mutually set with the patient and/or family. Goals shall be based on the nursing assessment and shall be realistic, measurable, and consistent with the therapy prescribed by the responsible medical practitioner. Patient education and patient/family knowledge of self-care shall be given special consideration in the nursing plan. The instructions and counseling given to the patient must be consistent with that of the responsible medical practitioner. The plan of care must be documented and should reflect current standards of nursing practice. [JCAH, 1981, pp. 118, 119]

The JCAH standards specify that documentation of nursing care shall reflect the patient's status. Nursing documentation should address the patient's needs, problems, capabilities, and limitations. Nursing interventions and patient responses are to be noted (JCAH, 1981, p. 119). For example, the nurse must have specific objectives and goals for patient education. These should be documented, and each succeeding note on the record should indicate the extent or lack of progress toward the goal.

This chapter points out problems in recordkeeping and offers guidelines for appropriate documentation. Some of the standards for these guidelines may not apply specifically to all health care settings, but they are important in general because they indicate the concerns in the field today.

It is easy to understand why nurses sometimes feel that if there has been no change in a patient's condition, it is not necessary to document daily. This can be dangerous, however, as it is in nursing homes when a false assumption is made that no change has occurred. Nurses must be astute in their observations and look for changes, no matter how subtle. A thorough evaluation of a patient's condition on admission, a periodic review of his or her status, and a statement of condition upon discharge definitely should be documented.

Nursing is an interpersonal process. It is characterized by the encounter between a nurse and a patient and by the transactions that take place between them (Orem, 1971, p. 155). The salient aspects of these transactions require documentation that is objective, current, complete, specific, and detailed with regard to observable patient behaviors. In 1980, Creighton identified several essential aspects of charting. Charting is evidence, and evidence includes things we see, hear, feel, or smell. A nurse can see a rash or pinpoint pupils or swelling; he or she can hear what the patient says or listen to rales in the chest; the nurse can feel cold, clammy shins or a lump in the breast; he or she can smell noxious urine (Creighton, 1980).

A nurse's schedule must allow time for proper documentation. Nursing care is neither casual nor unplanned. Documentation should be given equal attention, but too often in a busy day, it is not. As a result, physicians often pay little attention to nurses' notes, seeing them as incomplete, boring, and irrelevant.

Until recently, most nurses were taught a standardized format, according to which they made notes as follows:

- Good day or night
- Ate well
- Dressing changed—dry and intact
- Out of bed
- Appears well
- No complaints
- Dr. Smith in

The negative side might look something like this:

- Bad day or night
- Refused to eat
- Complained of pain
- Dressing wet—changed
- Apparently not good
- Dr. Smith in

What do those notations tell us? Do we know what a good or bad day means to the nurse who kept those charts? A patient who has been in critical condition, with unstable vital signs and constant unusual pain might have a good day, with only slight improvement. Those relative terms do not give an accurate picture of the patient's progress.

We also do not know what the phrase "dry and intact" means, nor are we given a description of the incisional area underneath. The "wet" dressing is equally uninformative.

Until recently, words like "appear" and "apparently" were standard terminology for nurses. It was supposed that such vague phraseology would protect nurses from allegations that they were making medical diagnoses. Lawyers have difficulty with terms like these precisely because they are so uncertain. They lead to questions such as these: Is the nurse really sure of what he or she saw? Could it have been something else?

Documentation must show continuity of care and must provide a clear, specific record of just what measures were involved. Was a physician called? What was done to attempt to solve a patient's problem? How did the patient respond to treatment? Was there a lack of response to nursing interventions? Was an evaluation done to determine the effectiveness of the nursing care plan?

The authors' experience in nursing and in law has been that documentation is weak in recording the follow-up measures and evaluation that are part of the nursing function. Nursing audits have also found this weakness in documentation. Nurses may perform all the necessary and appropriate steps in nursing care, but when such steps go unrecorded, it is assumed that they were neglected.

Proper and accurate documentation can, in many cases, absolve the health care practitioner from liability. For example, in *Engle v. Clarke* [346 S.W.2d 13 (Ky., 1969)], a court found no liability on the part of the institution when a patient died from hemorrhaging approximately 13 to 14 hours after surgery. In exonerating the defendant, the court relied heavily on the fact that the nurses' entries on the medical record included hourly progress notes, observations of abnormalities, records that the physician was contacted, and evidence that the nursing staff followed through on physician orders.

In other cases, a lack of documentation can imply to the court that specific tasks were not done. For example, in *Collins v. Westlake Community Hospital* [57 Ill.2d 388, 312 N.E.2d 614 (1974)], a patient who had broken his leg was placed in traction and, three days after admission, underwent amputation of the leg due to irreversible ischemia. The court examined the nursing documentation very closely for indications of whether nursing tasks were performed. The physician's orders instructed the nurse to observe the condition of the patient's toes; the first day, hourly comments were made on circulation in the toes. On the second night, however, no record was kept of such observations between 11:00 P.M. and 6:00 A.M. (when the foot was found cold and without sensation). The court thus held that there was no proof the nurses had followed the physician's orders, and ruled in favor of the plaintiff.

As the courts continue to discuss the role of documentation in proving care or indicating the lack thereof, it is important for registered nurses to be aware of development in the area. For example, what needs to be documented? Both the JCAH standards (1981, pp. 85–86) and the Medicare conditions of participation [42 C.F.R. 1024.45 (g)(4)] require clinical observations, including those of nursing personnel, to be recorded in the patient's record. These entries should be factual, objective, and accurate; they should

Recordkeeping

avoid opinion, personal bias, or characterization. The JCAH standards require pertinent, meaningful observations and specific information in nursing notes, including details about dosage of medications or gases administered, status of consciousness, and vital signs on entering and leaving units.

A primary and initial step in documentation is a thorough assessment of the patient so that all nurses involved with the care of the patient will have a data base from which to develop and implement goals and actions. Each health care facility can develop a format to meet its specific needs and to give nurses a full picture of a patient's changing profile from admission to discharge. Some questions that can further help the nurse with documentation are the following:

- What are the goals and nursing measures for the patient?
- What are the nursing interventions for which the nurse is responsible?
- What progress or lack of progress has been seen?
- What is the evaluation of the nursing care?

A nurse must always do his or her own charting. We also recommend that spaces not be left for filling in at a later time. This can make a record look as if it has been altered when an item is squeezed in between other notes. A chronological order is desirable, but there is no prohibition against a nurse's recording a pertinent item if she remembers it after the actual time of observation.

Nurses' documentations should specifically record observable, measurable, objective data that provide detailed evidence of a thorough process of assessment, evaluation of interventions, progress or lack of progress, continuity of care, and evaluation. Each member of the health care team must also read the others' notes so that a more unified care plan can be implemented.

In summary, documentation is essential for many reasons, and is included in standards of practice as necessary to quality care. It takes time to record correctly, and sufficient time must be allotted in a nurse's daily schedule for this important task. In-service departments must ensure that nurses are knowledgeable about documentation and about what to include. Particular effort must also be made to inform temporary staff personnel about the importance of documentation. Table 3-1 lists the general guidelines for documentation which may be applicable to any clinical practice situation.

Questions and Answers

The Medical Record Per Se

What is the status of the medical record as a legal document? In order to understand the current status of the medical record as a legal document, one must first understand that the legal interests of the hospital, the patient, and the physician are all affected by the medical record. Take, for example, the question of who has access to the documentation of a patient's care and progress. The JCAH standards and various state regulations provide that the medical record is the property of the hospital; that is, the hospital or the health care institution owns the medical record and may thus provide for reasonable avenues by which the medical record may be reviewed by another party or may be examined by the patient. Moreover, it must be recognized that the physician and the institution are obliged to maintain as confidential certain aspects of the information contained in the record. This further limitation of access has been upheld in a number of cases. In the case of *Gotkin v. Miller* [379 F.Supp. 859 (E.D.N.Y. 1974); *aff'd* at 514 F.2d 235 (3d Cir. (1973)], however, it was held that patients have a right to information contained even in their own psychiatric records. Subsequently, a line of cases has held that patients have a property right to the information contained in their records and should be allowed reasonable access. This right of access has been embodied in regulations in a number of states.

Physicians who are directly involved in the treatment of a

TABLE 3–1. General Guidelines for Documentation Applicable to Any Clinical Nursing Area

1. Know the procedures and protocols developed by your state or local health agency to encompass expanding nursing functions.
2. Know the joint rules and regulations of the nursing and medical associations.
3. Know the current nurse practice act of the state in which you practice and the rules and regulations developed under that act.
4. Know the ANA "Standards of Nursing Practice."
5. The assessment should be as complete as possible. It must be thorough since the nurse must base actions and decisions on it and chart these actions.
6. The nursing actions should be the kind that can be measured according to an acceptable standard of care.
7. The nursing actions should be based upon principles according to which they can be defended.
8. All the nursing actions should be charted.
9. All observations, nursing diagnoses, patient comments, and responses or lack of responses to treatment should be charted.
10. Everything done to follow up on observations, including responses or lack of responses to treatment, should be charted.
11. The chart should show that everything possible was done for the patient.

Prepared by LaVerne R. Rocereto, Ph.D., 1978.

patient also have a right of access to the record, whether as attending physician or consulting physician.

All these concepts of ownership, confidentiality, and right of access determine how the records will be used and by whom; but they do not alter the fact that the medical record is an official legal document and, as such, can be obtained by the various parties in a law suit and is admissible as evidence of the type of care given to a particular patient during hospitalization.

What data are included in the official medical record of an institution? The forms and formats used in medical recordkeeping may vary, but every record must contain information sufficient to identify the patient, to support diagnoses, to justify treatment, and to document the results accurately (JCAH, 1981, p. 84). Directives similar to this JCAH standard appear in many state regulations, and these too should be examined carefully in regard to the information that the medical record should contain—specifically, identification data, the patient's medical history, reports of any relevant physical examinations, diagnostic and therapeutic orders, evidence of appropriate informed consent, clinical observations including results of therapy, reports, procedures, tests and test results, x-rays, and conclusions at discharge or at evaluation and treatment. Every person involved in the care of the patient should be aware of what comprises the medical record in his or her institution. X-rays, for instance, are not attached to a patient's chart, but they are considered part of the medical record.

Who is entitled to access to a patient's medical record? Although various bodies may express it differently, the general rule is that information from medical records may be released to persons who have a legitimate interest in the information contained in the record and to those persons or parties for whom the patient has provided authorization. Of course, when a court order directs that a certain medical record be made accessible or a subpoena directs that it be produced in court, the patient's consent or authorization is not required. And if a hospital is sued by a patient, the hospital may use the medical record in its own defense. A hospital may also allow physicians on its own staff to consult medical records for research purposes, and it may use the records or their contents for purposes of statistical evaluation, research, and education.

A question has recently arisen over the right of outside academic or research groups to extract needed information from medical records and their right to use such information. The legal treatise writers appear to go both ways on this issue. Some state that the patient's rights are paramount and that the information should not be disclosed to an outside research body; others maintain that as long as the information is disclosed in such a way as to protect the patient's anonymity, the research group, with the approval of the institution, may examine the record for data-gathering purposes.

The Privacy Protection Study Commission, as established by the Privacy Act of 1974, has recommended that this type of information may be disclosed without patient authorization if the information will not be redisclosed in individually identifiable form. This commission further recommends that the patient's authorization not be required for a medical care provider to disclose information regarding a patient:

1. to another medical care provider who is using or will use the information in connection with the treatment of the individual;
2. to a properly identifiable recipient pursuant to a showing of compelling circumstances affecting the health or safety of an individual;
3. for the purpose of auditing or evaluating the medical care provider;
4. pursuant to a state or federal statute requiring disclosure, such as a law enforcement authority.

In general practice, however, most medical care providers obtain patient authorization before disclosing patient information to legitimately interested third parties such as insurance companies, attorneys, medical research and education groups, government agencies, and other medical care providers. In this situation, the health care practitioner should refer to the policy of the institution to find out what circumstances require an authorization for release of information.

We have discussed circumstances under which the hospital, courts, and outside interest groups can examine and use the information contained in a patient's medical record. Now let us look at the rights of the patient. It is a matter of generally recognized case law that the patient or the patient's legally authorized representative has a right to access to his or her medical record. Some states have even enumerated this right of access in codified form in a "patient's bill of rights." However, because the institution is the legal owner of the patient's medical record, it does have a right to require the patient to comply with reasonable enumerated procedures before being allowed access to the information. For example, different policies might apply to current patients' rights of access than to the rights of former patients. Nurses and other personnel must be aware of these policies and implement them carefully.

Health care professionals must also know their institution's policy in regard to release of information because the related regulations and laws are complex. For example, a whole set of federal regulations exist for the release of records relating to alcohol and drug abuse patients. Questions arise as to what actually constitutes a diagnosis of alcohol and/or drug abuse and under what circumstances these special regulations would therefore apply. These issues have been worked out very carefully by the administrators of individual institutions, and nurses should be cognizant of the policy as set forth in each institutional manual.

What is the correct nursing response to a current patient's request for access to his or her medical record? Let us repeat that it is important for the professional nurse to be aware of the institutional policy in this regard, particularly because most states provide a general right of access to patients. This does not mean that the nurse should merely hand over the medical record to a patient. Rather, the professional nurse on the unit should be able to react and respond to a patient in a manner consistent with hospital policy. He or she can tactfully inform the patient that such an avenue is available to the patient but that the physician should be consulted to review the medical record with the patient. A patient usually requests access to the record because he or she is confused about the type of hospital care provided.

Does a parent always have access to a minor's medical record? In the usual situation, the parent is considered the legal guardian of a minor and therefore has access to the minor's medical record. In addition, the parent is entitled to authorize the release to third parties of information contained in the record. Nurses should know the age of majority in their state. In most jurisdictions, it is eighteen years.

There are exceptions to this general rule that allow minors to give certain forms of consent and the right to authorize the release of information. These exceptions are granted for various reasons, such as marriage, being a high school graduate, or having ever been pregnant. In such cases, the parent would no longer be considered the legal guardian and would not have an absolute right of access to the medical record.

Certain other situations exist in which minors may be considered emancipated and therefore have the right to information contained on the record. Some states have recognized by legislation the minor's right to privacy in these areas. For example, in Pennsylvania the minor may consent to treatment for a communicable disease, for a pregnancy-related condition, or for a condition related to drug or alcohol abuse. As in the other situations, the minor's right to privacy would supersede the parent's right of access to the record.

In order to avoid controversy, it is advisable that the physician be notified when a parent seeks information. After checking state law, the physician may find it necessary to consult the minor patient and release the information in question only with the minor's permission. The physician should note this permission in the medical record.

When does the next of kin have a right to access of information contained in the medical record? The next of kin or legally authorized representative of a patient or former patient may have a right of access to information in the medical record when the patient is unable to assert his or her own right of access. For example, the parent or legal guardian of a minor or of a person adjudicated incompetent can assert such a right. The next of kin can also assert such a right after the patient's death, if he or she is the administrator or executor of the patient's estate.

In deciding when this right exists, we must first consider the patient's right to the record and then see if the next of kin can be placed "in the patient's shoes." The individual states assign the patient's rights to next of kin according to specific lines of descent. While observing state law, hospital policy will usually delineate who will receive the patient's medical record—the spouse, children according to age, or other relatives. In next-of-kin situations, a question always arises in an institution's medical records department as to whether the next of kin claiming the patient's right actually has that right. It is both the obligation and the responsibility of the institution to investigate whether the appropriate relative is requesting information and whether the patient in fact is physically, mentally, or legally unable to sign the authorization. When the hospital has reason to dispute the right of next of kin, verification by a notary public or the patient may be appropriate.

Does the patient have a right to amend or add to his or her medical record? This question is far from being settled. It poses many problems because if a patient were given the absolute right to amend or add to information in the record, that information could very well be incorrect and medically inaccurate. However, the law and regulatory bodies recognize that the patient should not only have access to the information in the record but should also be able to question the accuracy of that information.

The Privacy Protection Study Commission has thus recommended that any institution that maintains medical records should have a policy for possible amendment or addition to the record. If an individual feels that information contained in the record is inaccurate, the institution should contact the individual who made the entry and allow discussion between that person and the patient. Moreover, the patient should be allowed to add to the record a

Recordkeeping

statement explaining why he or she feels that the other facts it contains are incorrect. Each institution, however, may have its own procedures for adding or amending information, and each registered nurse should consult institutional policy on this issue.

Does an attorney have a right of access to information contained in a patient's medical record? Although a number of states have statutes that specifically permit the patient's attorney to inspect the patient's record, it is the opinion of the authors that the patient's written authorization should be required. Circumstances are different, however, for current patients than for former patients. Often, for instance, an attorney wishes to question a patient and review a medical record while the patient is hospitalized. In such a case, the nurse who works on the unit must remember that questioning a patient or attempting to review his or her medical records could jeopardize the patient's condition. Such requests must therefore be accompanied by permission from the attending physician as well as from the patient. Both authorizations should be entered in the medical record and signed by the physician and the patient. At that point, whether the nurse can allow the attorney direct access to the record becomes a matter of hospital policy. Such direct access is usually not allowed unless the physician is to review the chart with both the attorney and the patient present, thus preventing the possibility of later allegations that the attorney removed or altered part of the medical record.

In the case of a former patient, that patient's written authorization alone should suffice to allow the attorney access. Some hospitals also require the attending doctor's authorization, but the general trend seems to hold that the physician has no legal right to deny the patient's attorney access to the record. The physician's authorization is usually obtained merely as a matter of courtesy. Whether the entire record should be disclosed would depend on the facts and circumstances of the case, and it must be remembered that the outside attorney who requests access can always subpoena the records if he or she feels the necessity to do so.

Does an insurance investigator or an insurance company have a right to access to information contained in the medical record? Many third-party payers, such as insurance companies, Medicare, and Medical Assistance, have written agreements with institutions that provide for the release of certain patient information to the third-party payer. This information is usually relevant to the question of whether the level of care the patient received was necessary and whether the costs of the care were reasonable. Requests from insurance companies and others with financial interests in the records should, in general, be honored only with the patient's authorization. Many insurance companies incorporate such authorization into the policies as a condition of providing insurance. These broad authorizations usually pertain to medical information specifically requested for the completion and processing of standard insurance claims forms, and, in the normal case, medical records personnel require a separate patient authorization before releasing any additional information.

Of particular interest to the nurse is a question that may arise when an insurance investigator or representative arrives on the unit where a patient is currently hospitalized and asks to see the patient's medical record. Such requests should come only from the institution's central administrative office, not from these individuals themselves. Nurses should know who in the institution is authorized to grant outside investigators access to the medical records of former or current patients, and they should refer an investigator or insurance representative to this person.

Does any physician have a right of access to information about any patient? Only those physicians directly or indirectly connected with the treatment and care of a patient should have access to that patient's medical record or to any other information regarding that patient. Even if a physician works in the institution and is well known to the nurses on the unit, he or she should not have automatic access to information unless there is a reason to look at the chart. An example of such a case would be when the doctor is consulted with regard to that patient's treatment.

The Nursing Role in Patient Recordkeeping

What are the general guidelines for correct nursing documentation? When entering information in the medical record, a registered nurse must keep three concepts in mind: accuracy, objectivity, and relevancy. Documents characterized by these three attributes can be used for protection against legal liability, whereas documents that lack these qualities can more easily be interpreted as evidence that an appropriate standard of care was not followed.

Good nursing procedures can lead to good documentation. If we analyze proper nursing procedures, we see elements that involve assessment, planning, implementation, and evaluation. Recent use of nursing audits to evaluate patient care has shown that even if nurses conform to standards of practice, very little documentary evidence of those standards shows up in the medical record, leaving room for a lawyer or jury to assume that the standard of care was not met.

Documentation should follow the steps of good nursing. First, all data assessed should be included. Second, the record must detail the plan for care, and third, it should outline the nursing measures used to provide an adequate standard of care. For example, documentation should describe what the nurse is responsible for in the treatment of the patient, what progress has been made, and what regression has occurred. Fourth, the medical record should reflect the evaluation process; it should show that the nurse is continually seeking better ways to help the patient. It should show that the nurse is seeking options and alternatives, if necessary.

The nurse needs to state observable behavior while avoiding conclusion and diagnosis. The nurse might say, "The patient weaved back and forth and stumbled. The odor of alcohol was on his breath. His speech was slow and slurred." This description states facts about the patient's condition and behavior, but it does not venture a conclusion (that the patient was intoxicated) or a diagnosis (that he is an alcoholic). It provides information for both while leaving responsibility for both up to the physician.

We have noted the following on some charts:

10:00 P.M.	Dr. X notified about change in pt.
10:45 P.M.	Called Dr. X again and requested he see pt.
11:30 P.M.	Dr. X too lazy and indifferent to see the pt.

These negative notations give no indication of observable behaviors. The nurse, therefore, has no baseline data from which to determine a change in the patient who needed to be checked by a physician. This is frequently the physician's reason for not going to see the patient. Many physicians whom we polled indicated that when a nurse calls, he or she says, "The patient's condition is not good." When the doctor asks why, the nurse may respond with "He looks bad." These terms give no specific examples of changes in the patient's progress. A concise assessment of the patient's condition gives much more factual data. A better way to document would be the following example:

10:00 P.M.	Dr. X notified that lower left limb was cold, pedal pulse difficult to feel. Requested he see pt.
10:45 P.M.	Called Dr. X again. Lower left limb still cold; some mottled spots noted. Pedal pulse absent. Requested he see pt.
11:30 P.M.	Called Supervisor Y. Requested to have another physician see pt. stat.

Can specific nursing actions or observation be summarized on patients' medical records? In general, summarizing is not advised because specific actions or observations must usually be placed in the context of the patient's condition. For example, if a registered nurse is used to caring for very ill patients, her summary may differ markedly from that of a nurse who is used to caring for patients who are not acutely ill. Findings and observations that must be charted to back up an evaluation must also be included in a summary because a summary in the form of conclusions changes the

Recordkeeping

nature of the medical record from fact to opinion. Blanket statements and conclusions can easily be questioned and can be seen as diagnosis for which a nurse has no authority. A plaintiff's attorney can have a field day with blanket terms, generalizations, and conclusions in impeaching an attending nurse's testimony.

Should the nursing flow sheets and work sheets be retained as an official portion of the medical record? Any documents that indicate tasks performed for a particular patient by a health care professional should be retained as part of the medical record if those actions are not recorded elsewhere. Usually, such flow sheets and work sheets are the only record of a very closely timed sequence of a patient's care on a continual basis.

If a specific protocol exists for some type of nursing action, does a reference to that protocol constitute a sufficient entry in the patient's chart? If a policy and procedure or protocol exists as to a specific nursing task, it is appropriate merely to reference that protocol for a specific date and time on the patient's chart. However, it is important for the registered nurse to realize that he or she must follow the current policy or protocol and not an outdated one.

In addition, one must mark the chart and record every time such a protocol was followed as well as the exact time of day. For example, many institutions have a protocol or policy and procedure on decubitus care. Instead of charting each nursing measure and what a nurse does each time the decubitus care is given, it is sufficient to chart the date, the time sequence, and the nurse's observations on each occasion. It is especially important to describe accurately what the nurse observes each time the protocol is followed in order to determine the patient's progress or lack of progress.

How can a nurse minimize the possibility of someone's altering or adding to the nursing section of a patient's medical record? A nurse should not leave spaces or large blocks of space between entries in a patient's medical record. Sometimes a nurse will leave room for someone else to write what was done on the previous day. This is inappropriate. It must be remembered that nursing notes are the only written records of care that include both the time and date in strict chronological order. Because several persons will chart on each record, each must get his or her charting done promptly so that the record can be kept chronological. Registered nurses have been taught for a number of years to chart on consecutive lines on the record, but many nurses still chart on vacant lines or between lines to insert information. It is necessary to reinforce this basic rule of charting on consecutive lines with no space between various nurses' notes. If a note has been omitted and is out of sequence, it is advisable to chart the data in the next available space and to indicate the date and time period to which it refers.

How do I correct an error in charting? A nurse should determine whether the institution has a policy for correcting errors in charting. If so, he or she should follow that policy since it would be referred to as a standard by an opposing attorney. Usually, however, errors in charting can be corrected satisfactorily by crossing out the incorrect section, placing the corrected version as near as possible to the crossed out portion, and marking the correction with the nurse's name or initials and the date. The error should not be erased or completely obliterated. "White-out" material should never be used because it raises many questions if the record is ever reviewed by an attorney.

Is there a correct procedure for signing one's name to a patient's chart? Again, the nurse should inquire whether the institution has a specific policy. Usually, however, problems are minimized when a nurse signs his or her first initial, last name, and designation—R.N., G.N., L.P.N., or N.A. In this way, there is no problem later in determining the identity and designated status of the person who actually charted.

When is a cosignature required on a patient's chart? Cosigning by a physician or a faculty member is required for a number of activities done by various health care professionals, and indicates approval or ratification of the specific function or task that is charted. It also indicates that the cosigner verifies the correctness of the treatment or procedure. Cosignature is sometimes required by law and sometimes required by hospital policy. The cosignatures may not be required immediately; instead, they may be required within a specific period of time, usually 24 hours. Most states also require cosignature by a physician for verbal orders carried out by a nurse within 24 hours after the verbal instructions have been issues. In all cases, however, cosignature indicates awareness that the act was done and verification that it was appropriate.

When an untoward incident occurs, how should this be documented in a patient's record? It must be remembered that the health care professional is obliged to document every action performed and every response by the patient. The clinical observations, follow-up, and patient response, even in the context of an untoward incident, must therefore be entered in the record. If the patient falls out of bed, this must be recorded. It is inappropriate, however, to include any opinion regarding blame or assigning fault. Conclusions and opinions should not be placed on the record, nor should the fact that an incident report was filed. Only clinical observations, follow-up, and patient responses should appear on the chart in an objective, concise fashion.

When documenting a nursing observation, what additional information should be charted to complete the records? It is the experience of the authors that most nurses document observations adequately, but they fail to record what they did to complete the assessment process. For example, if a patient complains about having difficulty breathing, the nurse usually enters that fact in the chart, but the nurse very seldom documents what he or she does to follow up on that patient's problem. We recommend that the nurse note whether he or she called a physician, whether respiratory therapy was ordered, whether medication was given, and so on. All items must be on the record to show that proper continuity of care was followed and that a nursing evaluation was made.

Is the nursing assessment process an appropriate guideline for determining which items should be documented? We recommend that registered nurses use the nursing assessment process as a guide to correct documentation and as the best protection against possible lawsuits. The nursing assessment process enumerates the steps required for a proper, complete, and objective assessment of the patient. If a nurse goes through the entire assessment when recording correct patient care, the result should be effective and useful documentation.

Is it necessary to document general nursing care? The response to this question will vary with institutional policy. Some policies state that a general task, such as a bath, does not have to be charted unless a patient refuses it. We believe that the nurse's observation of the patient's response is more important than documentation of routine care. Instead of stating that morning care was given, the nurse could chart the following information: "Observed skin during bath. Some dry scaly areas on elbows and heels. Lotion applied."

A neglected area of documentation, in our opinion, is nutrition. Nurses do not usually see a patient's tray because dietary staff often deliver the meals and pick up the trays; further, the nursing staff themselves may take meal breaks while the patients are eating. It may not be necessary to check that all patients eat at every meal, but a systematic effort should be made once a day to monitor the amount of food consumed, especially by patients who, for physical or emotional reasons, may be less apt to eat. These observations of dietary intake should be recorded on the patient's chart. Particular attention should be paid to patients on restricted diets. Documentation should be made to aid evaluation and determination of any need for health teaching.

Protocols for areas of frequent nursing care, such as decubitus care, can be documented each time they are done, as follows:

    10:00 A.M.   Decubitus protocol followed.

Recordkeeping

A nurse's observations should all be recorded so that an evaluation of the patient's progress can be made each time. It is unnecessary to chart the entire protocol each time as long as a current, up-to-date protocol is part of the institutional policy and procedure so that it can be relied upon to indicate a standard of care.

Since "general nursing care" varies according to clinical areas and the needs of the patient, nurses in each unit should jointly review charting procedures and decide which routines need to be documented, which kinds of observations should be recorded, and how charting can be made more objective, consise, relevant, and meaningful. Inservice programs should be offered regularly to bring nurses up to date on new methods and goals of documentation designed to meet legal requirements and contingencies more completely and reliably.

Are letters, symbols, and abbreviations used in recordkeeping acceptable in good documentation? Letters, symbols, and abbreviations can obviously make a medical record confusing or hard to read. In the interest of avoiding misinterpretation, symbols and abbreviations should be used in the medical record only when they have been approved by the medical staff of the institution and when an explanatory legend is available to those who make and read entries in the record. Each abbreviation or symbol should have only one meaning (JCAH, 1981, p. 89).

Particular care must be taken in recording drug orders so that no mistake can be made in reading them. Abbreviations in this case should be used only when they are included in a legend that is part of the policy and procedures of the medical records department. A nurse should always check this official legend to see which abbreviations, symbols, and letters are acceptable. This enables the nurse to read the physician's orders correctly and to document accurately and clearly.

What members of the nursing staff might be required to document? Any member of an institution's nursing staff who is involved in direct contact with a patient might be required to document. This includes registered nurses, practical nurses, nursing assistants, student nurses, and private duty nurses. Documentation by each of these individuals is probably useful to the institution. Institutions do vary on this practice, however, so that it is necessary for the professional nurse to refer to institutional policy and procedure to find out who is responsible for documentation on behalf of the nursing staff.

Is the professional nurse assigned to a patient responsible for the documenting tasks performed by others? The trend in health care is to permit all health care professionals to document their own tasks on the patient's medical record. Some institutions, however, like professional nurses to be responsible for documenting the tasks performed by their subordinates. Registered nurses must therefore refer to their job descriptions and to the policy and procedure manual to clarify their responsibilities for documentation. It is the opinion of the authors that the person who performs the task and observes the patient should make the appropriate entries in the medical record.

The Role of the Individual Nurse in Institutional Recordkeeping

How do I document suspected unprofessional conduct or incompetency on the part of another health care professional? To whom do I report such a problem? A nurse who sees evidence of incompetence or lack of professionalism in a coworker should first find out if that person is a registered nurse employed by the institution. A nurse who makes a complaint about a peer is susceptible to question about her ability to identify unprofessionalism in a colleague. Grounds for judging a peer and avoiding such questions appear in some states' case law and in the rules of the nursing licensing board rules, or in previous opinions. Examples of grounds for an incompetence charge are as follows: misuse of drugs; improper delegation to persons not licensed as registered nurses; failure to exercise due care; any conduct, practice, or condition that may impair a nurse's ability to practice the profession safely and skillfully.

Grounds for a charge of unprofessional conduct are, of course, much broader; but they usually involve failure to comply with the code of ethics for nurses or with traditional standards of professional conduct. If, for example, an individual fails to maintain confidentiality in a given patient's case or falsifies records, the question of unprofessional conduct will certainly arise. Less clear cases might involve, for instance, the use of profane language or the irresponsible discussion of treatment methodologies with patients.

If an institution or a licensed registered nurse charges another licensed registered nurse with either unprofessional conduct or incompetence, the acts providing grounds for such allegations must be fully and objectively documented. This is sometimes very difficult to do, especially in ambiguous situations. It might be clear, for example, that a patient is not receiving his or her prescribed drug, but it may not be clear who is receiving it instead. An accurate ledger with times, dates, and detailed specific actions is obviously important and useful. It can even be advisable for an individual nurse to keep a private ledger.

Evidence of incompetence or unprofessional conduct not only should be recorded but should be reported immediately to one's supervisor, who is then obliged to investigate the problem. Supervisors and head nurses must realize this obligation and investigate charges of incompetence or unprofessional conduct discretely, quickly, and efficiently. Results and methods of investigation, such as a review of the medical record, must be documented; and any action taken against the accused registered nurse must also be recorded. The action taken must be consistent with the nursing department's policies and procedure and with the hospital-wide policies and procedures regarding infractions.

At this point, it may be necessary to report to the state nursing licensure board. In some cases, reporting is discretionary; in others, it is mandatory. The head nurse or supervisor must find out which infractions in his or her state must be reported and which do not require a report. The supervisor's objective, factual documentation of the case is extremely important. It should include witness statements, examples of inaccuracies on patient records, and long-term observations of the head nurse and others with times and dates appropriately recorded. Conversations with or questioning of the accused employee should also be documented adequately, along with any disciplinary action taken.

What responsibility does the nurse have to report apparently inadequate staffing? If the registered nurse finds himself or herself unable to function adequately in a certain unit because of insufficient staff, it is his or her responsibility to report that fact to the immediate supervisor. First, however, the nurse should be familiar with the staffing recommendations for his or her particular unit, which provide a rationale for the existing number of staff. Once the nurse has this information, he or she may then be able to show, by citing the complexity of patient needs, that there is a demand for health teaching or other necessities not provided for already and why more nurses are required. It may not be possible or practical to obtain the staff-to-patient ratio that an individual nurse deems essential, but a documented, well-thought-out plan to request more staff can be achieved. The nurse need not be silent on the matter of inadequate staffing.

Inadequate staffing is a common problem, especially when nurses, or funds, or both, are scarce; and an understaffed institution may be making a genuine effort to remedy the problem. It is important that the individual staff nurse notify the supervisor regarding the need for more staff or for a shifting of staff. This can be done verbally at first; but if inadequate staffing is a recurring problem, complaints to the supervisor should eventually be made in writing, following an appropriate form. Documentation should include an objective, factual description of the actual situation in which understaffing is a problem, noting the unit, the dates and times that problems arose, the number of patients, the types of problems requiring attention, and the number of nursing staff. Given this information, the supervisor can then form his or her own judgment as to whether the unit is inadequately staffed.

Recordkeeping

What general guidelines should a head nurse follow when documenting possible disciplinary problems? The documentation of employee problems or behavior, like the patient's medical record, should meet careful standards of objectivity, accuracy, and relevance. A head nurse should therefore avoid anything that compromises these qualities. He or she should not, for example, enter in the employee's records any conclusions not based on fact. To do so would undermine objectivity. Nor should the head nurse record any observations regarding the employee's private life; these issues are irrelevant. And, in the interests of accuracy, reports from one employee alleging the absence or incompetence of another should be recorded as such and not as direct observation. Supervisors must personally watch for possible problem areas and keep an ongoing record of employee behavior. Some nursing staff keep anecdotal files that are merely daily records of observations about employees. They are usually brief, containing a concise record of perceptions triggered by a supervisor's observation of an employee—for example, recurring patterns of absence or tardiness. Such anecdotal records can be used in evaluating employees and showing entire behavior patterns instead of isolated instances. This is fair to the employee, as long as documentation remains objective, that is, as long as both positive and negative factors are recorded and no personal bias is maintained.

A supervisor should also discuss both problems and strengths with the employee directly and confidentially. When a written evaluation is made, the employee should read it, discuss it with his or her supervisor, and sign it. The signature should not imply that the employee accepts the evaluation but should indicate that he or she has read and discussed the evaluation with the supervisor. The employee should be free to write his or her own comments on the evaluation.

The supervisor and head nurse have an obligation to understand and be aware of both the nursing department and the hospital's personnel policies and procedures. They should know how to implement these policies in their units and to be consistent with past policies and procedures in the institution. If questions arise, the head nurse and the supervisor should consult with the personnel department about past and current practice regarding a specific issue.

When a head nurse or supervisor does find it necessary to discipline an employee, he or she should do so progressively; that is, the head nurse should start with a verbal warning and mete out gradually more stringent reprimands and punishments if the offense continues. In fairness to the employee, the supervisor should not immediately follow a verbal warning with dismissal, unless the infraction is very serious. In response to the usual disciplinary problems, such as tardiness, absenteeism, or minor incompetence, the employee must be warned and disciplined progressively and in accordance with the policy and procedure of the institution.

When should the head nurse notify other department heads of potential risk problems? When should notification be in writing? Although most head nurses are highly competent in clinical practice, they generally do not work closely with other health care professionals in the institution; as a result, the institution suffers increased risks. To counter these risks, head nurses on a unit should be able to notify appropriate department heads of potential risk problems within their own units. Of course, before this can happen, the head nurse must be able to identify the risk, which in some cases he or she can do only if the institution has educated its nurses about its particular potential risks. Any problem or incident that exposes the institution to legal liability places it at risk, and a myriad of possible problems are capable of doing this. Equipment can fail, for example; a dangerous condition might exist on the unit; and questions of incompetence may arise about individuals who work in other departments but who come onto the unit.

These types of problems, if observed by the head nurse, should be brought to the attention of those individuals responsible for them. For example, if a particular type of equipment on the floor has failed or is in obvious need of repair, the proper maintenance department within the institution must be informed. The equipment should not be used until it is repaired. If a crash cart is placed on the unit without the proper equipment or with defective equipment, the head nurse should in this case notify the department responsible for getting the appropriate equipment on the crash cart. If persons who come on to the unit do not behave appropriately or show signs of incompetence, the head nurse must take the problem to the appropriate department head. These and similar steps minimize the risk potential of these problems. If, however, the appropriate department head or responsible party fails to act on a problem within a reasonable time, and if the situation continues, or recurs, then notification of the problem should be submitted in writing to the next-higher appropriate department head.

What records are considered part of the employee's official personnel record? Employee records are business records; they are admissible into evidence to show an employee's past performance on a job. They can also be used to rehire an employee or to consider an employee for promotion or advancement. Therefore, it is essential to enter in the record only those facts and objective observations that relate specifically to a particular employee. The official employee personnel record usually includes the employee's application, wage or salary information, any forms completed at the time of hiring, behavior reports, evaluations done in the course of employment, letters from supervisors or other employees, outside requests for information from the employee's file, and the termination notice. Usually, anecdotal notes kept in a private file by a supervisor or head nurse are not part of the official personnel record. Nevertheless, should a legal contest arise between the employee and the institution, the anecdotal notes would be admissible as evidence of a pattern of behavior and appropriate supervisory response.

Does an employee have a right of access to his or her own personnel record? The general trend allows an employee the right to the information contained in the personnel record. Some states have provided this right of access in statutes. Some institutions and employers have written policies detailing the procedures by which access can be obtained. An employee may usually review his or her personnel record in the presence of someone in the personnel office to ensure that items are not altered or removed. In most cases, the employee can also obtain copies of the record at reasonable cost. It is important for supervisors to understand their institution's policies and procedures regarding this right of access.

4
Interdisciplinary Practice Issues

Introduction

"The problems with the health care system today arise because there are too many people and too many jobs. It was much better when we only had to worry about the doctor and the nurse." This remark is all too common. Nurses and physicians often used to be the only members of a health care team. In America in the 1800s, many husband-and-wife teams worked as physicians and nurses in hospitals and clinics, and then social workers began to be added to the team.

Following World War II, massive changes occurred in health care services in America. In particular, the new technologies required more specialized personnel. From 1950 to 1975, the number of people employed in health care grew from 1,525,100 to 4,855,501 (Manpower Analysis Branch, Bureau of Health Manpower, 1978, p. VI–21). Health care workers now comprise more than 5 percent of the total work force. The largest single employer among the 150 industries monitored by the Department of Labor is the health care industry.

At first, this vast expansion and diversification in health care complicated matters of territory, leaders, communications, responsibilities, and legal roles. Many new issues and questions arose because each member of a health care team tended to be educated in a single, specialized discipline. Each knew little about the others' work, and had no opportunity to gain expertise outside his or her own specialty. Nurses, who comprise the largest single category of health care workers, tended to view each new health specialist as an invader of their turf. As a result of this situation, communications broke down, roles became ambiguous, jealousy arose, and competition increased. Interdisciplinary trust diminished, and few opportunities remained for exchanging or broadening knowledge and expertise.

In the past decade, greater attempts have been made to coordinate the efforts of each discipline, to increase compatibility, and to deliver a more integrated system of care to clients. Interdisciplinary and multidisciplinary collaboration have encouraged teamwork. Multidisciplinary teams are mixtures of health and social welfare professionals from diverse disciplinary backgrounds. Interdisciplinary teams also include professionals from diverse backgrounds, but these team members usually work at the same site. The collective identity of an interdisciplinary team is more important than the individual status of each of its members. This chapter focuses on issues in interdisciplinary care that can create problems for nurses.

Although we cannot cover the subject in detail here, it is essential for nurses working in interdisciplinary teams to be completely familiar with the range of function and responsibility of each team member. This familiarity is basic to a thorough understanding of the nurse's role and rights in carrying out orders of the health care staff other than a physician. For example, chiropractors, osteopaths, podiatrists, and clinical psychologists are sometimes extended staff privileges in health care facilities and hospitals, and yet a nurse who follows their orders may, in some states, be in violation of the professional nursing law. Some of these laws state specifically that a registered nurse may execute orders of a licensed physician or dentist. An osteopath generally is considered to be a licensed physician, but the question of whether nurses can take orders from chiropractors, podiatrists, or clinical psychologists should be decided by each state's board of nurse examiners.

Each nurse must be familiar with the relevant laws of the state in which he or she is employed.

One of the newest members of the interdisciplinary team is the physician assistant. This discipline emerged in about 1965, when Duke University started the first two-year program for former military corpsmen. At first, most physician assistants worked in rural clinics. Now they are being employed in urban and suburban clinics, acute care facilities, and so on, coming into contact with increasing numbers of nurses.

State statutes vary, but physician assistants generally act as delegates or agents of a physician. They are usually permitted to write medical orders and prescribe certain types of drugs. This can raise questions for nurses over carrying out the physician assistant's orders. Because the physician assistant is viewed as the agent or delegate of a physician, some states—through opinions issued by their attorneys general or by judicial decision—hold that the nurse must follow the physician assistant's orders as if they were the orders of a physician.

In states that mandate the execution of orders from a physician assistant without a physician's countersignature, a nurse must still determine if the institution has authorized such a policy, because the institution has the power to set certain constraints upon a physician assistant's practice. The nurse should also question any order that seems to be erroneous or ambiguous, and the nurse has the right to refuse to execute such an order.

Many nurses are unwilling or uncertain about questioning unclear or incorrect physician's orders, and they are unaware that they can legally refuse to execute these kinds of orders. They still believe that blind obedience to the physician is the route a nurse must follow. Moreover, it is not unusual for nurses to be told by their supervisors that refusal to carry out orders is grounds for dismissal.

Unfortunately, these beliefs have been reinforced in the past. Nurses were told that they were to be faithful servants to the master (the physician). Loyalty to the physician was the primary duty of nurses (McAllister, 1955, p. 325). This kind of advice implies that the patient's welfare was a secondary consideration or that it could best be served by unquestioning obedience to the physician. It is essential for professional nurses and nursing students to realize that the law protects them if they have legitimate reasons for refusing to carry out an order and if they report their actions immediately to the line supervisor so that steps can be taken to ensure the safety and welfare of the patient.

The Nightingale Pledge states that the nurse will not knowingly administer deleterious drugs. The American Nurses' Association's Code of Ethics of 1976 emphasizes that the nurse must safeguard the client and the public when health care and safety are jeopardized by incompetent, unethical, or illegal acts.

In recent years, more new jobs have been created in each health care discipline by training technicians to assist professionals. This proliferation of jobs at all levels can compound problems for a nurse, who is often the only one with round-the-clock responsibility for the patient. This does not mean, however, that interactions among disciplines need to be chaotic and counterproductive. A few guidelines can help to minimize the possibility of interdisciplinary conflicts and subsequent litigation.

Competence in one's own area of expertise is a major prerequisite to harmonious interdisciplinary teamwork (Ducanis & Golen, 1979). The majority of nurses are professionally competent, but many tend to feel inadequate when they relate to an interdisciplinary team. Too often they say, "I am just a nurse. What can I do when a physician (or physiotherapist or social worker) will not listen to me?" This readiness to assume a passive, dependent role is a detriment to accountable and legally defensible nursing care. It is professionally acceptable for a nurse to be sure of her own job and expertise and to refuse to assume the role of any other health care provider in his or her absence. A nurse who is confident of his or her own skills and position can help the whole team avoid the blurring of roles that leads to the nurse's taking over when no one else is there. The nurse must perform within the scope of the nurse practice act and not be every other professional's "Man Friday."

Meetings in which communication and problem sharing take place are helpful. It is important, however, that all members of the health care team avoid taking, or making, criticisms personally and that an adversary relationship between individuals or disciplines give way to cooperation.

The ANA Code of Ethics needs to be clearly understood. A survey of ethical codes of other health professions revealed five major topics covered by them: professional competence, relationships with colleagues, relationships with clients, legal responsibilities, and relationships to society (Golen & Ducanis, 1977). While this professional code is legally enforceable only if it is part of the nurse practice act, it offers every nurse a guideline to behavior with peers, clients, and colleagues. Ducanis & Golen (1979) raise the question of whether members of each profession should be trained in the ethical standards of other professions in order to avoid interprofessional conflict. We recommend that nurses at least read the codes of ethics of other health professions to gain a better appreciation of their purposes and their implications for nursing.

A commitment to the continual development of interdisciplinary relationships will ultimately result in a unified standard of practice that will minimize risks to the patient or client. Such a commitment should be the goal of every health care professional.

Questions and Answers

What is the nurse's responsibility in executing physician orders? In most states, the definition of professional nursing specifies that the nurse must execute medical regimens as prescribed by a licensed physician or dentist and, in most instances, the nurse is protected by a physician's order. There are circumstances, however, in which a nurse may question such an order—for example, when the order is manifestly wrong or the nurse knows that the physician is not qualified to give that particular order. The nurse must, therefore, assess the situation independently to determine within the scope of his or her nursing practice whether the modality of treatment is correct. If, under those conditions, the nurse feels an order is manifestly wrong, he or she has a duty to so inform the physician and, if an order is ambiguous, to obtain clarification from the physician. If the physician does not respond or explain in such a way as to dispel the nurse's doubts, the nurse has a duty to inform the supervisor or head nurse that he or she believes the order is wrong.

In responding to orders given by physician assistants, nurses must know the role that physician assistants have been given within their particular state. Most states that have laws regarding physician assistants in their medical practice acts allow them to give orders to nurses and other health care professionals. However, these laws are usually in contravention or conflict with the Professional Nursing Law, which says that the nurse may follow only those orders given by a licensed physician or dentist. In some states, this question has gone as far as the attorney general's office or the courts themselves. In Washington, for example, the physician assistant has been deemed an agent of the physician, and the nurse is therefore expected to follow the physician assistant's orders as if they were orders of the physician [Washington State Nurses' Association v. The Board of Medical Examiners, Sup. Ct. Opinion No. 46148, 1980]. A number of other states have generated the same opinion through their attorney general's office [Michigan Attorney General Opinion No. 5220, 1977; Iowa Attorney General Opinion No. 78-12-41, 1978]. In each case, when the physician assistant has been allowed to give orders in place of the physician, the nurse must refer to the institutional policies and procedures regarding the physician's orders. If the institution allows the physician assistant to give orders, the nurse should still follow an order only if it is not manifestly incorrect.

When should a nurse refuse to carry out a physician's order? When a registered nurse, in applying his or her education and expertise, believes that an order is erroneous or ambiguous and when a physician does not dispel the nurse's belief that the order is wrong, the nurse may refuse in the following fashion to carry out the physician's order: the nurse must inform the head nurse or supervisor that he or she questions the order and must describe the reasons.

It is the hospital's duty to create a system in which the nurse is not caught in an ethical web. The supervisor or administrator must get involved to discern in which manner medical attention should be given to the patient. If the nurse does not do so, he or she is still obliged to refuse to carry out an order that is manifestly wrong. For example, if a physician prescribes a medication to which the nurse knows or believes the patient to be allergic, the nurse should withhold the medication. All observations that lead to the nurse's refusal to follow orders must be documented, including notification to the physician and the appropriate supervisor of reasons for questioning the order.

Such documentation should not be entered in the patient's record in a way that implies criticism; it is sufficient to say that notice was given. If, however, the problem is not resolved, an objective memorandum to the supervisor is in order. The nurse should include in this type of memorandum the objective facts of the situation, at which point the supervisor is obliged to investigate and attempt to ameliorate the conflict between the physician and the nurse.

In some states, professional nursing law requires a nurse to carry out orders prescribed by licensed physicians or dentists. What medical practitioners are included in this group? Although recommendations have been made on a national basis, this question has usually been decided by licensure boards in individual states. In Pennsylvania, for example, nurses are allowed to carry out orders prescribed by a licensed physician, dentist, or osteopath. Most states have also ruled that a nurse can take orders from a chiropractor, but only if the chiropractor is a member of the hospital staff.

How should a nurse document a refusal to follow physician orders? Refusal by a registered nurse to follow a physician's orders may occur only if the nurse reasonably believes the order is manifestly wrong or that the physician is imcompetent to give such an order. The facts and observations leading up to such a refusal must be documented. First, any relevant and particular patient problems should be noted. If, for example, a patient claims that he or she is allergic to a particular medication, that statement is part of the nursing assessment process and must be placed on the medical record. The physician should also be notified of this additional fact, at which point it would be appropriate for the nurse to refuse to follow a physician order and to notify his or her supervisor of the refusal. The refusal itself need not be entered on the record because lack of documentation indicates that the task was not completed. It is appropriate, however, for a nurse to submit a separate chronological memorandum to the supervisor detailing the events surrounding, and the reasons for, a refusal to carry out a given order. In this way, the nurse protects himself or herself from possible disciplinary action and other consequences.

How should a nurse react when a physician does not respond to notification of a patient problem? It is always appropriate to document instances in which a physician is notified of a patient problem and to note the time and nature of notification. In an extreme emergency, when the notified physician has failed to respond, it is appropriate for the nurse to obtain help from another physician as quickly as possible; patient care comes first. When a choice is possible, however, a slower course of action may be acceptable. For example, the nurse may decide to notify the supervisor instead of taking action personally, in which case it is up to the nursing supervisor to act on the problem. If the supervisor fails to do so within a reasonable time, however, the nurse must once again decide where to take the problem and whether it warrants higher administrative attention.

In every case, the whole chronology of events must be written up in an objective memorandum to the appropriate supervisor, who should then act on the problem in a reasonable fashion. It is inappropriate to include criticism or subjective conclusions in the medical record. These are irrelevant to the patient's care; they do not constitute objective facts.

How can a nurse differentiate between a medical diagnosis and a nursing diagnosis? The definitions of professional nursing in various states exclude functions traditionally considered within the practice of medicine—for example, medical diagnosis and prescription of treatment. Nursing diagnosis, as distinct from medical diagnosis, refers to the nurse's responsibility to determine whether a matter is within the scope of nursing practice or requires referral to a physician. The case of *Cooper v. National Motor Bearing Company* [136 Ca.App.2d 229, 288 P.2d 581, 51 A.L.R.2d 963 (1955)] involved an action against an industrial nurse for negligence because she failed to probe a wound or to refer the patient to the physician when the wound did not heal. The central issue in the case was whether the worker was contributorily negligent in failing to consult a physician. The court ruled that he was not because he had relied on the judgment of the nurse.

Nursing diagnosis is expanding the nurse's role. This is still an area under study but a number of states have included some mention of the nursing diagnosis in their practice acts. Some states expressly prohibit diagnosis by a nurse; others fail to mention diagnosis as a physician's exclusive perogative. Many states that clearly forbid diagnosis and prescription of treatment on the part of a nurse are presently considering revision. And in those states that do allow nursing diagnosis, one must find out exactly what that term means. The language is likely to be vague. For example, in Pennsylvania, a portion of the practice of professional nursing is defined as "diagnosing and treating human response to actual or potential health problems" [63 P.S. §212(1)]. And in New York, Pennsylvania, and other states, diagnosis means the identification of and discrimination between physical and psychosocial signs and symptoms essential to the effective execution and management of a nursing regimen [New York State Education Law Op. Title 8, Art.

139 §6901]. Most nursing writers recommend that a nursing diagnosis be understood to emerge out of the nursing assessment process rather than out of any assessment process learned by physicians.

Is it within the scope of nursing practice for a nurse to express an opinion that is different from the physician's about the patient's condition? In regard to a particular function or task that is within the scope of nursing practice, a nurse may make an opinion independent from that of the physician. In fact, many state practice acts oblige nurses to make such independent nursing judgments about patient care. Common law holds the nurse responsible for tentatively diagnosing a patient's condition in an emergency and, in the absence of medical help, for taking whatever measures are necessary (Willig, 1970). Many cases can be cited in which nurses were held liable for a failure to diagnose and act. In some cases, a physician may decide within his or her own realm of medical judgment that the nurse's preliminary diagnosis was incorrect.

Nurses have always observed phenomena and have used the nursing assessment process in caring for patients, and they have made judgments and decisions based on multiple data. Thus, nursing diagnoses and opinions regarding medical care merely demonstrate the cognitive ability to appraise a situation, to draw conclusions from the appraisal, and to act on the conclusions (Bullough, 1980, p. 90). A physician's diagnostic function, on the other hand, focuses on determining the cause and the most effective treatment of a disease. Nursing diagnosis simply identifies symptoms and attempts to discover a means for alleviating them.

What should a nurse do when a physician gives the verbal order "Do not resuscitate," but will not write this order on the patient's medical record? Case law provides that a DNR order, written by a physician for a terminally ill patient whose family agrees to this order, is a valid order that may be executed by the hospital staff [Matter of Dinnerstein, 380 N.E.2d 134 (1978)]. The nursing service department should, therefore, obtain a directive from the medical staff regarding policy and procedure in this area. Physicians can be informed of the legal validity of this type of order by a multidisciplinary committee made up of nurses and physicians in the hospital. In this way, the nursing services department may obtain cooperation from physicians. Many physicians prefer to write the order in the Kardex Nursing File, which is not part of the medical record. When this happens, the nurse should write what the physician told him or her to do in the nurse's notes.

Medical staffs have begun to take firm stands on the written DNR. For example, Presbyterian University Hospital, at the University of Pittsburgh Medical Center, has a clear set of guidelines for intensive care units to follow in terminal cases, one of which states unequivocally that the physician must write a DNR. This has removed the nurses' dilemma of what to do when it is not a written order.

What sources should a nurse consult in order to differentiate between nursing and medical practice? All registered nurses licensed in a particular state are obliged to examine that state's professional nursing law and its accompanying rules and regulations, which will include the definition of nursing in that state. The nurse must then learn how rigid or flexible the institution that employs him or her is in interpreting the state's definition. Although the functions and definition of nursing are expanding, many of the issues involved are being interpreted by state boards or joint boards comprised of physicians and nurses, by states' attorneys' general offices, and in the course of judicial decision making. In regard to sensitive issues, nurses must examine the relevant state laws with particular attention.

If a nurse is asked to perform a task that is outside the scope of nursing practice, how should he or she respond? If one has reason to believe that a function or task one has been asked to perform is outside the scope of nursing practice, the appropriate response depends on the situation. If the patient is in an emergency situation (that is, if delayed action could cause a loss of life or limb), the nurse must act quickly and effectively. Appropriate actions in this case might include immediate performance of nursing procedures and the calling in of other staff to handle the problem without direct physician approval. When there is time to exercise a choice, however, it is more appropriate to bring the issue to the attention of the nursing supervisor, who might be able to deal with the physician in an administrative capacity. The nurse is still accountable if he or she undertakes activities that the law does not permit him or her to do.

Is the registered nurse responsible to the patient or to the physician? As an independent licensed practitioner in a given state, the nurse's primary obligation is to the patient or client within the proper scope of nursing practice. Within that scope, the nurse has the obligation to execute orders and medical regimens as prescribed by a physician or dentist; in other words, the nurse must follow the physician's orders unless the nurse has reason to believe that they are in conflict with the patient's welfare or with the nurse's responsibility to stay within the proper scope of nursing function. The nurse is responsible to bring to the attention of the physician observations and changes in patient condition. The nurse also is responsible for the continual care and monitoring of the patient. In some circumstances, the physician may be responsible for directly supervising the nurse, as an anesthesiologist would supervise a nurse anesthetist. In such cases, the nurse must get the physician the information needed to perform in that kind of supervisory capacity. It must be remembered that a registered nurse's primary obligation is directed to the patient or client.

What is the nurse's role in patient education? Patient education should be viewed as the mutual responsibility of many health care disciplines. This interdisciplinary approach recognizes that different aspects of patient education are performed better by one health care professional than by another. In most states, however, patient health teaching or health counseling is enumerated as one of the independent functions of nursing, so it is important to see this independent function in relation to other health care professionals.

We suggest that this role of a health teacher or health counselor is a permissive function of nursing and that the nurse must therefore find out what the particular institution expects and allows in terms of patient education. What is to be taught to the patient and who is to teach it should be decided in each institution in terms of the permissible tasks of health care professionals and the constraints placed upon those tasks by other disciplines. The institution should decide the nurse's specific role in health teaching and health counseling even though the nurse practice act may allow it. A multidisciplinary committee should develop a list of tasks to be performed by each health care provider in the institution, including the nurse's educational tasks. For example, education regarding therapeutic diet may be shared by the dietitian and the nurse.

Is it necessary for a nurse to obtain a physician order before contacting a social worker for a particular patient? In many institutions, it is customary for a social worker to be assigned to every patient. In others, the social service department is available for consultation with every patient. If a nurse observes that a patient needs social service intervention, it may be appropriate for a social worker to become involved, in which case the nurse would not need a physician's order before making that contact. If, however, the nurse becomes aware of facts about the patient that may require a physician's attention for a related medical or psychiatric problem, it is imperative that the nurse inform the physician of those facts. The physician may then decide whether to work more directly with a social worker on the case.

Are guidelines available for the registered nurse that delineate responsibility in relation to other health care professionals? State licensure bodies and associations representing health care professionals have determined a need to clarify the responsibilities these professionals have to one another. A coordinated effort to define or delineate those responsibilities has been made. For example, in a number of states, the functions that a nurse practitioner can legally perform have been jointly promulgated by the nursing licensure board and the medical licensure board. In other cases, professional associations and state boards have issued joint statements regarding particular accountability levels in different professions and under specific circumstances, such as those surrounding inhalation therapy or the handling of drugs. If a particularly sensitive issue arises in an institution, the nurse should first refer to state law and regulations and to those of the professional associations to see if a joint statement has been made. If not, the nurse should take the issue to an inhouse multidisciplinary committee and ask for clarification of responsibility from them. Clear definitions of responsibility should exist for all health care professionals so that questions regarding responsibility do not continually arise.

Is it permissible for a registered nurse to go to the pharmacy after hours to secure a medication unavailable on the unit? Many institutions have a 24-hour pharmacy service or have established a unit dosage system, but there are still instances in which the registered nurse has to secure a medication that is unavailable on the unit. If the medication has been ordered by a physician, and if a pharmacist is available in the pharmacy, it is permissible for the R.N. to go to the pharmacy and pick up the medication for proper administration to one patient. However, this policy should be reviewed by administration.

It is inappropriate for a nurse to go to the pharmacy and draw up or dispense the medication himself or herself. The pharmacist, whether in the hospital or elsewhere, has the sole responsibility for dispensing medications either for individual use or as floor stock, "dispensing" being defined as the issuing of one or more doses in a suitable container, such container being properly labeled by the dispenser as to the contents and directions for use.

Is it permissible for a registered nurse to delegate the task of administering medications to another member of the nursing team? In most states, the administration of medications falls within the exclusive realm of the registered nurse or, sometimes, the licensed practical nurse. This authority is granted by the professional nursing law, and its delegation in special circumstances is usually referred to in a given state's regulations. The registered nurse must read very carefully that section of the regulations dealing with the administration of medication; it will usually state how administering a drug may be delegated. In most cases, the responsibility may be delegated only to a nursing student in an approved program or to a graduate nurse who has not yet been licensed by the state. In each case, the individual who has drawn up the medication must also administer it. It is not permissible for the R.N. to allow anyone else to draw up medication in a syringe that the R.N. will later administer.

Are there any restrictions on the types of medications that a nurse may administer even though they are ordered by a physician? Professional nursing laws provide in general that a nurse may administer drugs, but a particular institution or doctor may decide it is not in the best interest of the patient or the nurse for the nurse to administer a certain type of medication. For example, the physician may wish to administer the first dose of an experimental drug to a patient who has not received it before. This is a particularly common practice with chemotherapeutic drugs because the physician can immediately detect any initial adverse reaction.

Questions regarding drug administration should be addressed either to the pharmacy and therapeutics committee of a specific institution or to a committee of physicians and nurses set up to formulate the policy on administration of medications. Institutional restrictions may be established on the types of medications a nurse may administer. Every nurse is expected to know of any such restrictions in his or her institution.

Who is responsible for giving respiratory therapy treatments if they are ordered after the respiratory therapist has gone home? The overlapping of responsibility between the respiratory therapist and the registered nurse has been an unclear issue. In some states, joint regulations or joint statements have been promulgated by the respective licensing bodies and the professional associations of both groups. In states with such a joint statement or joint regulation, nurses should find out whether the statement specifies who is to provide respiratory therapy if a respiratory therapist is unavailable.

In most states, the registered nurse may administer therapy as ordered by the physician. Nevertheless, administration of the therapy has to be approved by the institution through written policy. Moreover, the registered nurse must have instruction and practice in using the equipment and must have demonstrated his or her competence to either an inhouse committee or some other body responsible for monitoring the administration of the therapy. A nurse who is asked to administer respiratory therapy when a respiratory therapist is not available should refer to his or her institution's policy regarding the proper training in the equipment and methods used. We believe that the nurse should not have to substitute for the respiratory therapist; he or she is the one who has been educated and skilled in these techniques. The respiratory therapy department should assume its rightful role by staffing to meet the patient schedules.

What is the proper course of action for a nurse to follow after specific instructions or directions have been given to a particular patient by a physical therapist? The practice of physical therapy requires highly specialized training and education. The nurse should be told what specific instructions have been given and how the nurse can reinforce those instructions in the care of the patient. This is a case in which members of two disciplines can exchange necessary information about a patient so that complementary action can result. If a nurse does not understand the instructions or feels the patient may be confused, the nurse should call the physical therapist to discuss these concerns.

This question refers to one of many instances in interdisciplinary health care in which proper communication and a sensitive willingness to clarify ambiguities can result in higher-quality patient care and increased health team cooperation. When one or both parties are defensive, an impasse can occur, with fragmentation of care. The patient is caught in the middle. (Please note that physical therapy is used as an example here in a question that could apply equally to many other specialty areas.)

What is the obligation of the registered nurse working on a unit to communicate a patient's problem to appropriate other departments? We can safely say that if a nurse knows that a particular patient is experiencing a problem, it is within the proper scope of nursing practice for the nurse to assess that problem and notify other health care professionals. For example, if a patient has a degree of hearing loss, the nurse should communicate this fact to someone who can logically be expected to treat the patient for it, or whose treatment of the patient for another condition might be affected by the knowledge. If a patient has been highly sedated, for example, physical therapists should know this fact before they begin therapy. This type of communication contributes to higher-quality patient care and reduces the risk of the patient's suffering unduly from the problem in question. When other departments have been notified of the problem, that notification should be entered on the record.

What is an appropriate course of action for a nurse to follow when he or she suspects incompetence in a health care professional other than a nurse? No particular health care professional has the right or authority to decide what correct practice is for other health care professionals. Nevertheless, in some cases, a problem can be unmistakable to a health care professional even from another field. When it is, that professional has the obligation to the patient to ensure that the behavior and performance of the suspected professional is being carefully monitored. If a nurse observes a clinical action that he or she feels is inappropriate, it is the nurse's prerogative and duty to inform the nursing supervisor. In so doing, the nurse must relate only relevant, accurate facts. If the supervisor does not act immediately, the nurse should submit a written communication to the supervisor, whose responsibility it would then be to communicate with the supervisor of the other health care professional. Under no circumstances, however, should a nurse communicate personal doubts to nursing peers, to the patient, or to peers of the other health care professional.

5
Independent Liability

Introduction

In the past, the law viewed the nurse as an agent of the hospital or physician and only infrequently held the nurse directly accountable for any acts of negligence. In the past decade, there has been an increasing emphasis on the nurse's liability for his or her own professional actions. The new roles that have emerged in recent years—for example, those of the nurse practitioner and the independent nurse practitioner—carry and will continue to carry new responsibilities and corresponding new liabilities.

Nurses were formerly taught that most of their functions were defined by the physician's prescribed orders and the nurse's dutiful execution of those orders. Too often, nurses still operate according to this notion, and the nurse who wants to be independently accountable is sometimes viewed, with suspicion and mistrust, as a divisive figure. We have given seminars to countless nurses who still assume that they are not liable because they are responsible only to the institution for which they work.

The independent functions of a nurse are determined by the nurse practice act; the individual nurse's level of experience, expertise, and education; and the scope of practice defined according to local and national rules, regulations, and standards of practice. Some independent functions of the nurse are:

1. to apply the nursing process to patient and client care;
2. to observe, report, and document the signs and symptoms of the patient or client;
3. to develop a nursing diagnosis for the patient or client, the nursing diagnosis being the process that identifies the patient's resources and deficits, thus indicating his or her needs for nursing assistance; and
4. to supervise and coordinate auxiliary nursing personnel and to determine their level of competence when assigning them to patient or client care.

In general, the nursing profession recognizes the need for independent liability, but there are still factions that hold differing views. Corless (1980, p. 141) identifies the professionalizers as those who advocate the advancement of the occupation. The traditionalizers, on the other hand, continue to view the nurse primarily as someone in a dependent role whose major function is to carry out the physician's orders.

The functions of a physician and a nurse sometimes overlap, but some components of patient care belong exclusively to one or the other. When the phrase "independent nursing function" was introduced, many people understood it to mean that the nurse was completely free of the physician's influence. All nurse practice acts, however, hold nurses accountable for executing the orders of licensed physicians or dentists as long as the orders are correct. They also provide for a broad range of nursing functions that can be done independently. The health care system should clearly maintain that the physician is responsible for medical care; the nurse is responsible for nursing care; all other health care professionals are responsible for their own areas of expertise; but all must function interdependently in order to accomplish the goal of providing quality care to patients and clients.

Every nurse must accept the necessity of making nursing judgments. A nurse can no longer remark that he or she does only what the doctor orders. Such an approach to nursing is not within the scope of nursing practice, nor is it legally defensible.

Nursing judgments must evolve out of the steps of the nursing process. In this way, the nurse can demonstrate that he or she has made intelligent nursing judgments from a solid data base. Inadequate data collection based on bias, casual observations, and subjectivity can lead to improper judgments.

An example in which a nurse made a casual observation based on insufficient data is *Citizens Hospital v. Schoulin* [48 Ala. 101, 262, So.2d 303 (1972)]. The nurse manipulated the legs of a patient who complained of back injury and numbness after an accident. In a telephone conversation with the physician, she stated her opinion that the patient had been drinking and that nothing was wrong. The next day, at another hospital, fractured vertebrae and paralysis were diagnosed.

Hearsay and superficial examination offer little of the kind of data needed for making correct nursing judgments. The nurse who is willing and able to make a nursing diagnosis and nursing judgment, and who insists on this right as a partner on the health care team, is generally capable of being a full colleague with members of other disciplines while taking independent responsibility for his or her own nursing actions.

Questions and Answers

The Staff Nurse

In what situations can the licensed professional nurse be held individually responsible? When a nurse exercises independent judgment and decides the course of action in a given situation, he or she can usually be held responsible for its outcome and can be charged with negligence if problems arise that can be traced to that judgement. When a nurse is charged with negligence or malpractice, however, the action is usually also brought against the physician, the hospital,

Independent Liability

or both. The patient's attorney thus attempts to prove liability in some respect against one or all of these defendants.

In the performance of professional duties, a nurse is required to exercise ordinary or reasonable care against unnecessary harm coming to the patient [Ybarra v. Spangard, 25 Ca.2d 486, 145 P.2d 687, 162 A.L.R. 1258 (1944)]. As stated in Chapter 2, the nurse may be held to a community standard, especially in the case of a regular unit nurse [Wood v. Miller, 158 Or. 444, 76 P.2d 1963 (1938)]. Nurse specialists, however, can be held to a standard of care established for their specialty according to national regulations [Webb v. Jorns, 473 S.W.2d 328, Tx. Civ. App. (1971) *rev.* at 488 S.W.2d 407 (1972); later appealed 530 S.W.2d 847, Tx. Civ. App. (1975)]. In any type of negligence action, the basis for liability is in tort (a private or civil wrong or injury; a wrong independent of contract). The patient's attorney must address four classic elements in order to prove negligence. The attorney should establish what the nurse's duty was in the situation being investigated and must then prove breach of duty, proximate causation, and the damage or injury resulting from the breach. Such proof must be established by expert testimony or by standards of practice introduced. In matters involving a nurse's use of judgment, expert testimony is required [Leonard v. Watsonville Community Hospital, 291 P.2d 496 (1956)].

What is the difference between a nurse's independent liability and a nurse's responsibility as an employee of an institution? Whether an institution is sued because of an employee's act or the employee is sued as an individual, the same four classic elements are required to prove negligence. In the past, a nurse employed by an institution was an independent contractor when performing nursing acts, but was an employee when performing clerical or ministerial acts, in which case the institution became responsible under the doctrine of *respondeat superior* (a Latin term meaning "let the master answer") [Schloendorff v. Society of New York Hospitals, 211 N.Y. 125, 105 N.E. 92 (1914)]. In the modern view, however, the hospital as an employer is automatically and vicariously responsible and liable for the negligence of its employees. In cases involving institutions as employers, the nurse, as employee, is usually not named individually in the suit. When the nurse is independently liable, however, he or she is named as a defendant in the lawsuit, and questions of insurance coverage may arise. It is important, therefore, for nurses to find out from their institution's insurance carrier what types of coverage are available to them if they should be named individually in a lawsuit. Coverage may vary from state to state and from carrier to carrier. It is a common tactic for patients' lawyers to bring all possible defendants into a lawsuit because multiple defendants may divide the interest of the various named parties.

What specific nursing tasks carry the greatest legal risks? Nursing tasks that belong exclusively to the realm of nursing seem to carry the greatest risk that nurses will be named as party defendants. We will attempt to discuss some of these situations here, but in no way will we be able to examine every possibility.

The only case we have found that involves a nursing diagnosis is that of *Cooper v. National Motor Bearing Company* [136 Cal. App.2d 229, 228 P.2d 581, 54 A.L.R.2d 963 (1955)]. In an action against an industrial nurse for negligence in failing to probe a wound or to refer the patient to a physician after the wound did not heal, the court stated that the standard of learning, skill, and care for nurses administering first aid would require the nurse to decide whether it was within her ability to treat the condition and, if it was not, would require that the patient be sent to a physician. In the *Cooper* case, a skin cancer developed on the patient's forearm, and the nurse was held responsible because she did not refer the patient to a physician.

Many cases deal with the nurse's duty to interpret and carry out orders properly. In *Larrimore v. Homeopathic Hospital Association of Delaware* [181 A.2d 573 Del. (1962)], a female patient had been receiving injections of a drug over a period of time, and the physician wrote an order to change the route of administration and to give the medication orally. When a nurse who had been off duty for a few days started to give the patient the medication by injection, the patient reminded the nurse of the physician's new order. However, the nurse told the patient that she was mistaken and gave the medication by injection. Because the nurse had failed to review the order sheet after being told by the patient that the medication was to be given orally, the court held that the nurse was liable for the resulting injury to the patient. In another case, *Norton v. Argonaut Insurance Company* [144 So.2d 249 La. Ct. Appeals (1962)], a nursing supervisor who had been pressed into duty on a pediatric floor misinterpreted a physician's written medication order. She thought that an injection was ordered, rather than a less potent and newly available elixir form of the drug. The nurse, believing that the medication order was incorrect, asked two physicians present in the unit whether the medication should be given as ordered by the attending physician. The physicians did not interpret the order as the nurse did and did not share the nurse's concern. The nurse administered the medication by injection without consulting the physician who had written the order, and the patient died from too high a dosage. The nurse was held liable for failing to consult the attending physician before giving the medication. (The physician who had written the ambiguous order was also held responsible.)

Other lawsuits arise out of the nurse's duty to monitor patient behavior continually, applying the nursing assessment process in order to observe abnormalities and irregularities and to inform physicians of them. The frequently cited case of *Darling v. Charleston Community Memorial Hospital* [211 N.E.2d 253 (1965)] best illustrates the importance of this duty. In that case, a seventeen-year-old football player with a broken leg was taken to an emergency room, where the physician cast the leg too tightly. The patient complained of discomfort, and his toes were dark, swollen, and without sensation. The nurses knew the symptoms as signs of gangrene and noted these symptoms in his records, but no medical staff member was notified. The hospital was held responsible for the nursing staff's failure to monitor and follow up on the patient's condition adequately.

The improper administration of an injection is another source of legal action. For example, in the case of *Budgen v. Harbor View Hospital* [2 D.L.R. 338 (1947)], the patient died after receiving an injection of Adrenalin that should have been Novocain. Neither the doctor nor the two defendant nurses had read the label. The court held that the prosecution did not have to show that the negligence of any single defendant was the cause of the death, but, looking at the entire situation, the negligence of one of the defendants caused the death of the plaintiff. In other cases, the institution has been held responsible for a wrongful injection by a nurse where the use of a nursing judgment was in order. For example, a nurse in one case failed to exercise correct nursing judgment when she used a standard length needle to give an intramuscular injection to an obese patient. The injection went into the subcutaneous tissue instead of into the muscle tissue and resulted in necrosis: subsequent surgery was required to remove sections of the patient's buttock.

Nurses have also been held responsible for the general safety of patients on the unit. If a nurse witnesses negligence by another health care professional that can seriously harm a patient, the nurse should halt the procedure in question or otherwise intervene to protect the patient. The physician also has a duty to intervene in such instances. When the situation that involves possible negligent conduct is not an emergency, the nurse has a responsibility to inform the supervisors of the other person's negligence so that the resulting dangerous condition can be rectified. A number of cases hold nurses responsible for failing to give proper attention to a patient in walking or getting around a unit or for placing equipment in a way that causes injury to the patient. For example, in the case of *Oldis v. La Société Française de Bienfaisance Mutuelle* [130 Cal.App.2d 461, 279 P.2d 184 (1955)], physicians, nurses, and the hospital were all held responsible when a patient sustained third degree burns on his abdomen after a major operation, even though it was not determined which defendant's negligence actually caused the burns. During the period in question, the patient was semiconscious and under the influence of pain-relieving drugs. There was some evidence that the nurses were negligent in applying too-hot water bottles to the plaintiff's abdomen. Many other cases point to the nurses' general responsibility in looking after the patient's safety and well-being and in taking into account the patient's state at the time, considering, for example, if the patient is senile, highly sedated, emotionally overwrought, and so on.

What other bases are there, besides professional liability, for bringing a nurse into a case as an individual? Without proving that a nurse has deviated from his or her duty or fallen below a certain nursing standard, a patient's lawyer may still be able to prove that the nurse is generally (as opposed to professionally) liable or has committed an intentional wrong against the patient. Many cases that do not specifically involve nursing malpractice do not even make this distinction, but a negligence claim against a nurse can be based on a general safety practice or on other factors that are within a layman's common knowledge. If, for example, in feeding a patient, a nurse spills coffee on him and causes severe burns, it may be proven that the nurse was serving the coffee negligently. The nurse would be held generally, not professionally, liable.

Most legal problems involving institutions arise out of negligence, but a nurse may also be held responsible for intentional wrongs. In those cases, it is not usually necessary to prove physical damages. Cases of intentional wrong may include libel, slander, false imprisonment, assault, battery, and invasion of privacy. Although nurses are seldom involved in such cases, the ones that occur usually do so if a patient or a patient's family is incensed over an action they consider highly unreasonable. For example, charges of false imprisonment and of assault and battery can be made when a patient is restrained. Nurses must therefore understand what hospital policy is in regard to the use of restraints. When is a physician's order required? What types of restraints can be used without a physician order? How should the use of restraints be documented? The answers to these questions will help a nurse to show that a given restraining action was reasonable and served the safety or welfare of the patient.

Nurses should also be aware of the new privacy rights afforded patients, particularly in cases where privacy is a major concern. Some states have statutes dealing with the minor's right to privacy regarding treatment for communicable diseases, drug and alcohol abuse, or pregnancy-related conditions. In these states, nurses should know how to handle a minor's right to privacy when a parent or guardian seeks to intrude on it. Nurses should also investigate their institution's policy and procedure regarding the release of information to the media. Unless they are aware of such guidelines, they may be open to invasion-of-privacy suits for wrongfully releasing information to the media or to other third parties outside the institution.

We do not intend to cover these situations fully in this section, but to draw attention to their importance and to the fact that nurses should be sensitive to the needs of the patient. When nurses must act against the patient's basic right to privacy, they should document the reasons for doing so.

Who can be held responsible for a patient's lost or damaged belongings? Most institutions have a disclaimer of liability for lost, stolen, or damaged items brought onto their premises. Patients are generally advised not to bring valuables into institutions because if they are lost or damaged, responsibility usually cannot be established, nor can the value of the items be proven. However, if the institution places valuables in a safe or otherwise attempts to maintain control over them, and if they then become lost, the institution may have some responsibility, which some case law likens to that of an innkeeper. A nurse does not usually have responsibility for items damaged, stolen, or lost on his or her unit. Of course, if a nurse damages an item himself or herself—for example, in taking the jewelry off a patient—he or she may be held liable. It is thus important for a nurse to find out if hospital insurance or personal liability insurance covers the nurse in such a case if a lawsuit arises.

Is it appropriate for a nurse to write physician orders if a physician dictates them? Although this request is commonly made by physicians, and although nurses are required to execute physician's orders, it is nevertheless inappropriate nursing practice to write the orders down as a physician dictates them. If a nurse writes them down in the medical record, he or she exposes himself or herself to liability for an error in dictation or in interpretation.

What is the appropriate response of a professional nurse who is temporarily assigned to a specialty unit? Many professional nurses who are competent as staff or general duty nurses do not feel competent to work in specialty areas, especially if they have not received inservice education in that specialty. The institution, of course, has the right to assign nurses to those units as needed, but such temporary assignments do not require the nurse to perform every task in that specialty unit. On the contrary, the nurse should, in the interest of the patients, inform the head nurse or supervisor that he or she is not competent to do certain tasks or to operate certain equipment or machinery. The nurse would thus protect the patients' safety and would also protect himself or herself against disciplinary action for refusing the specialty assignment; in addition, the nurse would protect himself or herself from any possible liability for wrongful or incompetent action.

When a nurse is assigned permanently to a specialty unit, how should he or she insure that personal competence is adequate for the necessary specialty tasks? The appropriate assignment of employees to various units is a joint responsibility of both the institution and the employee. In many states, the professional nursing law and regulations, along with the ANA and Joint Commission of Accreditation of Hospital standards, are very stringent in this regard. For example, there are numerous training requirements designed to insure a nurse's competence to use defibrillating or monitoring equipment, and similarly specialized procedures have equally strict requirements. Thus, nurses who are assigned permanently to specialty units must be aware not only of pertinent state laws or regulations, but also of ANA and/or JCAH guidelines that apply to that specialty. When guidelines exist regarding the level of competence required for a specialized task, the nurse must not perform that task until he or she has attained that level of competence. If in any case a nurse is uncomfortable about a specific procedure or device, he or she should inform the supervisor so that the supervisory staff and institution can upgrade the nurse's competence. In general, if a nurse has the training necessary for a particular procedure or device, the supervisor will assume that the nurse is competent in that regard.

Does the extent of the nurse's independent responsibility change with the situation in which the nurse works? Permissive and mandatory nursing functions as defined by state regulations do not change with the settings in which they are performed. But because different settings can carry different job descriptions, independent responsibility may change accordingly. For example, a nurse working in an acute care setting, surrounded by professionals from many disciplines, would not have the discretion and judgmental independence that an industrial nurse or a home health care nurse would have. In fact, the rare legal case questioning a nursing diagnosis involves an industrial nurse [Cooper v. National Motor Bearing Company, 136 Ca.App.2d 388 P.2d 581, 51 A.L.R.2d 963 (1955)]. Thus, it is important for a nurse to know not only the rules and regulations of a particular state regarding registered nursing as an entity, but also the professional guidelines for a particular specialty and the job description according to the nurse's place of employment. In addition, a nurse who works in various settings should know what his or her professional liability insurance covers. Insurance companies take different stands on this issue, and companies employing nurses have different types of policies. It is in the nurse's own interest to obtain a letter from the insurance carrier describing the scope of the nurse's employer's coverage, the nurse's own coverage, and any gaps in that coverage.

Is it within the scope of professional nursing to guarantee a patient's right to confidentiality and privacy? Action may be brought against a hospital, a physician, and/or a professional nurse when a patient believes reasonably that his or her right to confidentiality and/or privacy has been breached. The revised ANA Code for Nurses (1978) states that the nurse safeguards the client's right to privacy by judiciously protecting information of a confidential nature. This code is intended as a guide in the practice of nursing that is consistent with ethical rather than legal principles. However, in a lawsuit based on confidentiality or right to privacy, it could be admitted into evidence as an ethical standard for the nurse. The professional nurse does have a duty to protect and safeguard the right to confidentiality and privacy of an individual patient, but this does not mean the nurse can guarantee that right.

A nurse must be sensitive to a patient's need for confidentiality and privacy and must honor the confidential physician-patient relationship. The nurse should know to whom and in what manner information can be released, what constitutes proper authorization for its release, and what information is considered confidential.

What is the difference between a patient's right to confidentiality and the concept of "a privileged communication?" Confidential information in general is that which should not be disclosed to unauthorized parties. Privileged communication, on the other hand, refers specifically to a court rule of evidence. Not all states recognize the concept, and it varies among those that do; but privilege usually refers to the right of patients to object to their physicians' testifying in court about matters relating to their medical treatment. Originally, the concept of the privilege applied only to information shared by the physician and the patient; it was intended to promote trust between them. The privilege now has been extended to medical and hospital records, including entries made by nurses and others associated with the patient. Thus, one might assume that this right or privilege exists for the nurse and the patient also; but in court of law, only the patient may invoke the privilege of confidentiality since it is intended to protect the patient (Cazalas, 1978, p. 155).

A common question is whether privilege extends to general discussions between a patient and the health care provider. It is well known that physicians have an ethical duty not to disclose information they receive from their patients; nurses have that same duty. In most jurisdictions, information furnished to the physician is seen as privileged only if it is necessary to his or her ability to treat the patient.

Many states allow the physician-patient privilege to be invoked only in certain kinds of legal actions, excluding criminal proceedings and cases in which, for example, a will or administration of an estate is at issue. Some states recognize qualified privilege, under which concept a judge can require disclosure when he or she considers it in the best interest of the public. Usually, privilege can be applied to those parts of the medical record that relate to the treatment and care of the patient. A patient who sues a hospital or physician for negligence waives his or her right to invoke privilege.

What is the nurse's role in interpreting and ensuring the patient's bill of rights? In 1972, the American Hospital Association issued *A Patient's Bill of Rights*. Today, many states have promulgated such bills of rights as part of the rules and regulations for their own departments of health. Some of these regulations require each health care facility to have in place a bill of rights that does in effect guarantee certain rights to patients. These bills of rights have caused much confusion among hospital administrators and scholars because terms such as a right to privacy, confidentiality, and current and complete information are open to interpretation. Nevertheless, the patient's bill of rights clearly places on the hospital a

Independent Liability

responsibility for ensuring these rights. An individual nurse also has an obligation to learn both what state law is regarding a patient's rights and how a particular institution has decided to implement those rights. Many institutions give patients a patient handbook upon admission, and that handbook explains the patient's rights in layman's language.

Nurses should know how to implement certain sections of the patient's bill of rights adopted by their institutions. If, for example, the bill states that the patient has the right to access to information contained in the record, the staff nurse must know what to do when a patient requests such information. The nurse should be familiar with the policy and procedure of his or her institution; and if there is no appropriate policy, the nurse should seek instructions from the nursing administrator.

Should a licensed professional nurse carry individual liability insurance? A registered nurse should find out if a given state requires the nurse to obtain professional liability insurance. Most states do not have such a requirement. Even though nurses who work in institutions are usually covered by their institutions' insurance, they should find out how far that coverage goes. Does it extend to nurses who are sued individually? If a nurse is named in a lawsuit, does the coverage extend only to legal costs? Does it cover judgments or settlements? These questions can be answered by the employer or the employer's insurance carrier. Some companies do offer professional and personal liability insurance for nurses and such coverage can usually be obtained inexpensively through professional nursing associations, and sometimes as a rider to a home owner's or an automobile liability policy. We recommend that nurses carry their own liability insurance. Institutional liability policies might, for example, provide legal counsel for a nurse who is named in a malpractice suit, but leave the nurse to pay any judgments against him or her. For this reason, we consistently emphasize the importance of obtaining specific written details of coverage.

Does the good Samaritan statute in a given state protect a nurse in an emergency situation? Almost every state has "good Samaritan" laws that protect registered nurses who stop at the scene of an accident (Kelly, 1976). Nevertheless, many nurses who are aware of the good Samaritan statutes are not aware that they really do not owe any duty to a patient until care is requested and undertaken. This is merely a legal fact, however, and a nurse may feel that he or she owes an ethical duty to a person needing care. Fortunately, because of this legislation, the nurse is generally relieved from liability in rendering care in an emergency, except for acts amounting to gross negligence or willful and wanton misconduct. The statutes usually allow the nurse to give emergency care without requiring the nurse to provide follow-up care all the way to another site, such as a hospital, or until another person can take over. Some states even extend this protection to inhospital emergencies. Every nurse should refer to the good Samaritan law in his or her state to see what scope of protection is afforded in the emergency situation.

The Managerial or Supervisory Nurse
When is a nurse independently responsible for actions that occur in the areas he or she supervises? As a general rule, the nursing supervisor or managerial nurse is responsible for the functions specified in the job description and for problems that come to his or her attention or that should come to his or her attention in the reasonable performances of duty. When an act of negligence occurs, liability therefore may extend beyond the individual involved in the incident to include the person's supervisor. The doctrine of *respondeat superior* holds that an employer is responsible for the wrongful or negligent acts of employees (Perry, 1978). The nursing manager may also be held responsible because his or her supervision of employees in a given unit determines the general quality of patient care. Professional nursing laws identify the supervision of personnel as one of the functions of professional nursing, and failure to supervise in accordance with the standard expected of a professional nurse can constitute negligence. Any professional

nurse is responsible for the actions of those working under his or her direction or supervision. In addition to responsibility for direct supervision, the nurse manager is also responsible for ameliorating problematic situations, such as those arising from inadequate nurse staffing.

In what way is the nurse responsible for identifying potential or actual problems in the areas he or she supervises? Legal responsibility for quality patient care and patient safety is usually placed upon the hospital corporation. The nurse manager, however, is responsible within the hospital corporation for monitoring patient safety and maintaining quality care in the units supervised. Every nurse supervisor should find out from his or her own supervisors just what responsibility exists in this regard. Even general staff nurses and unit supervisors who are notified of a potential problem in patient care or safety can be responsible for acting to improve the situation; but nursing supervisors and nurse managers in particular must understand their responsibilities in that regard. The supervisor, for example, may play a key role in identifying potential risks to the hospital corporation. He or she may also be responsible for communicating these problems to administration or to other appropriate department heads for corrective action. Later in this chapter, we discuss the nursing supervisor's responsibility for knowing his or her place in the organizational structure and how to use that structure to communicate problems and to initiate corrective action.

Does the responsibility of a nursing supervisor or managerial nurse extend beyond the concerns of patient care? Nursing supervisors are often well aware of clinical standards of practice but uncertain how to identify or solve problems in other areas that may come under their responsibility. It is essential for this reason that they know exactly what responsibilities are outlined in their job descriptions and also just what position that job occupies in the institution's hierarchy of responsibility. A supervisor can thus discover what the reporting mechanism is within a particular institution and how he or she can interface with departments outside the area of nursing.

The nurse manager is accountable not only for the quality of nursing care in a given unit, but also for other duties specified in the job description. In a given nursing department, for example, it may be the managerial nurse's duty to formulate and enforce departmental policies. And because those policies are usually the first source a patient's lawyer consults regarding the institution's standard of practice, they must be constantly updated and improved. If, for instance, a nurse informs a supervisor that he or she finds the policies unworkable, the supervisor should see to it that the necessary changes are made.

Nursing supervisors must also be familiar with personnel policies and procedures. They must know how to document personnel problems and, to do so, they must know the state's definition of the proper scope of nursing practice and the institution's interpretation of the state's view. They must also know whether particular functions of nursing are mandatory or permissive so that they can enforce and interpret the institution's limitations on practice. Nursing supervisors have to handle employee grievances and must work in conjunction with their personnel departments. They are also responsible for carrying out the safety practices of the institution and must be able to communicate quickly with the maintenance or safety department to correct possible safety hazards. Finally, they must be able to fulfill all their obligations without stepping out of their place in the organizational structure, thus correcting problems and addressing difficulties without generating misunderstanding or confusion among other departments or the medical staff.

What are the nursing manager's individual responsibilities within the institution's larger hierarchy of responsibility? Supervisors and managers must know the various levels on which they may be held accountable for actions that occur in their areas of responsibility (see Figure 5–1). They may be held vicariously responsible through the doctrine of *respondeat superior* for the acts of persons

A. **For Acts of Subordinates**
B. **As Express or Implied Agent**
C. **Ostensible Agent of Institution**
D. **Independently**
E. **Corporate Liability: Indemnification**

FIGURE 5-1. Levels of Potential Liability for the Managerial Nurse or Nursing Supervisor
© copyright Cynthia M. Maleski, J.D., 1980

working under them. Or they may be held responsible as a stated or implied agent of the hospital, in which case the institution may in turn be held responsible for the supervisor's actions. If, for example, a supervisor is negligent in carrying out an institution's policies and procedures or in informing patients of their rights, he or she may be liable as an agent of the institution. If the supervisor is held responsible as an ostensible agent of the institution, the institution may be held vicariously responsible for the supervisor's acts, even if it did not grant the supervisor authority to perform the task at issue. If, for example, a supervisor explains a certain procedure or policy to a patient who then chooses care or treatment based on that explanation, the supervisor has acted ostensibly on behalf of the institution, and the institution can therefore be held responsible, as can the supervisor if the act were negligently performed.

Supervisors can be held independently responsible, especially when they have been notified of a potentially hazardous situation or are aware of conditions leading to one. If, for example, a staff nurse repeatedly brings an understaffing problem to the supervisor's attention and the supervisor does not attempt to improve the situation, a basis exists for an independent liability charge. Moreover, because the hospital or institution can be held responsible for a nursing supervisor or manager acting as its agent, the hospital has the right to bring an action for indemnification against such an agent who is found to be at fault in a situation that the hospital could not have been responsible for improving. This is rarely done, but the right to indemnification does exist.

Because of the various levels of accountability that exist within an institution, nurse supervisors must know their own position in relations to the others in an institution. Figure 5-2 shows a simple organizational structure. The board of trustees at the top of the chart is ultimately responsible for the hospital corporation, and members of the board delegate that responsibility through the administration and the medical staff. The nursing department usually reports to the board through the administration, and the managerial nurse or supervisor would therefore act as that department's representative to the hospital administration. A supervisor who keeps the schematic chart in his or her mind will understand personal legal accountability within the institution and will be able to assess potential legal risks both to himself or herself and to the institution per se.

How does this organizational structure affect a nursing super-

Board of Trustees

↕ ⋯⋯**Medical Staff**

Administration

↕

Managerial Nurse or Nursing Supervisor

↕

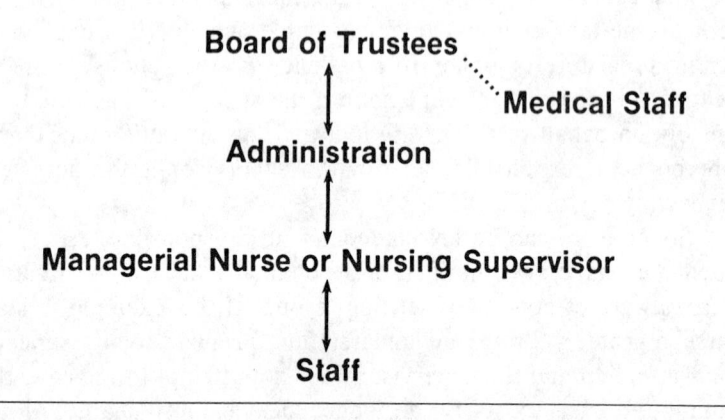

Staff

FIGURE 5-2. Legal Accountability within the Institution
© copyright Cynthia M. Maleski, J.D., 1980

Independent Liability 115

visor's relationship to the legal standards of care that have been discussed throughout this book? As Figure 5-3 points out, the supervisor's first duty is to be aware of the standards of practice within his or her own department and to know the correct standards of patient care and nursing practice in a given state and institution. Then the supervisor must set up, implement, and enforce proper guidelines through policy and procedure so that subor-

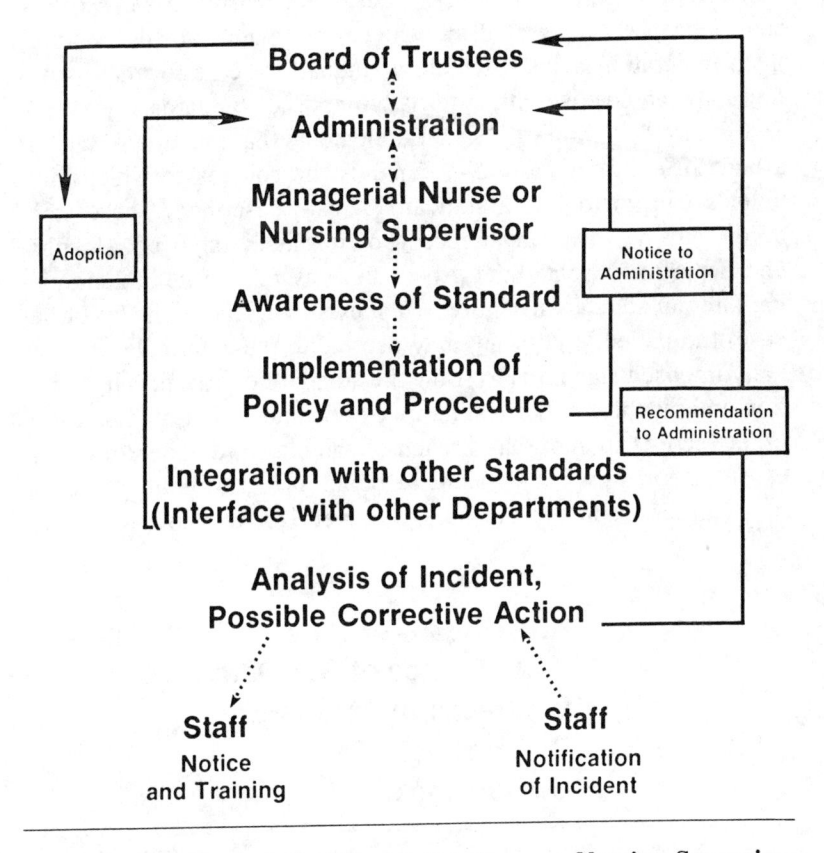

```
                    Board of Trustees
                          ↕
                    Administration
                          ↕
    Adoption        Managerial Nurse or        Notice to
                    Nursing Supervisor         Administration
                          ↓
                    Awareness of Standard
                          ↓
                    Implementation of
                    Policy and Procedure       Recommendation
                                               to Administration
                Integration with other Standards
                (Interface with other Departments)

                    Analysis of Incident,
                    Possible Corrective Action

              Staff                    Staff
              Notice                 Notification
            and Training             of Incident
```

FIGURE 5-3. Duty of the Managerial Nurse or Nursing Supervisor in Relation to Legal Standards of Care
© copyright Cynthia M. Maleski, J.D., 1980

dinates will know how to act in specific situations. The administrative staff in a given institution must then approve and adopt those policies and procedures. Such administrative approval is paramount because nursing units do not exist in a vacuum, and policy and procedure must be integrated with the standards of other disciplines. Thus, it is the duty of the director of nursing to bring to the attention of other administrators or the medical staff the policies and procedures within his or her own department so that they can be properly integrated into the entire organizational structure. Such integration helps to create a standard of care for the institution that can coexist with externally imposed standards.

Figure 5-4 shows the general elements that must be proven in a plaintiff's case. Figure 5-5 expands the sources to which individuals can go to find a standard of care described. These standards may be externally imposed or internally imposed. Hospital and department policy and procedure play a key role in determining internal standards. Figure 5-6 shows that, in proving his or her case, the patient's attorney may use either the externally or internally imposed standards to show the standard of care for an institution and may use either testimony or documentation on medical or other records to show the breach of the standard. Therefore, it is essential for a proper standard to be adopted and implemented in an institution and for the nursing supervisor to know his or her

A. **Standard of Care**
   1. **Source of Standard**
B. **Breach of Standard**
C. **Proximate Cause**
D. **Damages**

FIGURE 5-4. General Elements That Must Be Proven in a Plaintiff's Case
© copyright Cynthia M. Maleski, J.D., 1980

Independent Liability

Externally Imposed Standards
- **A. Statutes: State and Federal**
- **B. Regulations: Administrative Agencies**
- **C. Codes of Behavior, Conduct by Professional Associations and Accrediting Bodies**

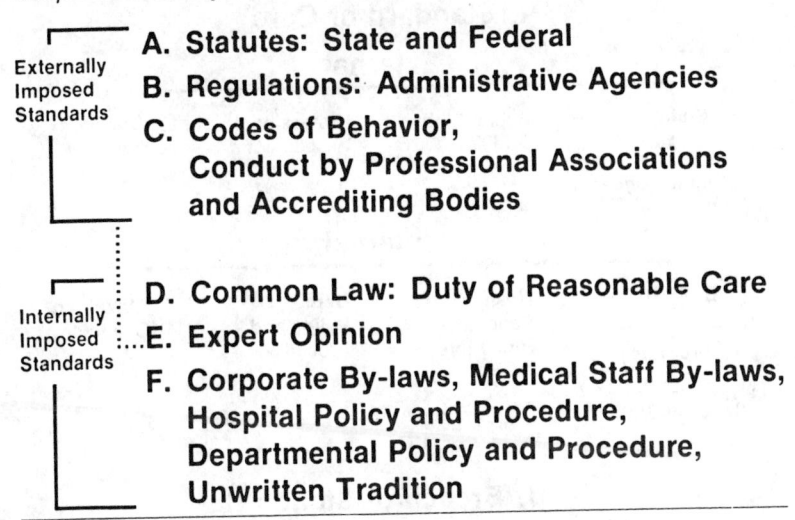

Internally Imposed Standards
- **D. Common Law: Duty of Reasonable Care**
- **E. Expert Opinion**
- **F. Corporate By-laws, Medical Staff By-laws, Hospital Policy and Procedure, Departmental Policy and Procedure, Unwritten Tradition**

FIGURE 5-5. Sources That Define the Standard of Care
© copyright Cynthia M. Maleski, J.D., 1980

responsibility for familiarizing staff with the policy and institution's organizational structure. As a last step in preventing legal risks to the institution, nursing supervisors must be alert to situations that compromise or fall below either the externally or internally imposed standards.

This discussion has now gone full cycle because the nursing manager can recognize such an incident only if he or she is aware of the proper current standards of practice, both internally and externally imposed. Unfortunately, the supervisor's duty does not end with identifying a problem. To do so, of course, the supervisor must know the proper channels for reporting such incidents and recommendations in a given institution. If no such channels exist formally, the supervisor should report such problems to the immediate supervisor so that possible corrective action can be taken. Figure 5-3 shows how such a reporting mechanism might arise. It examines the duty of the managerial nurse or nursing

A. Standard of Care

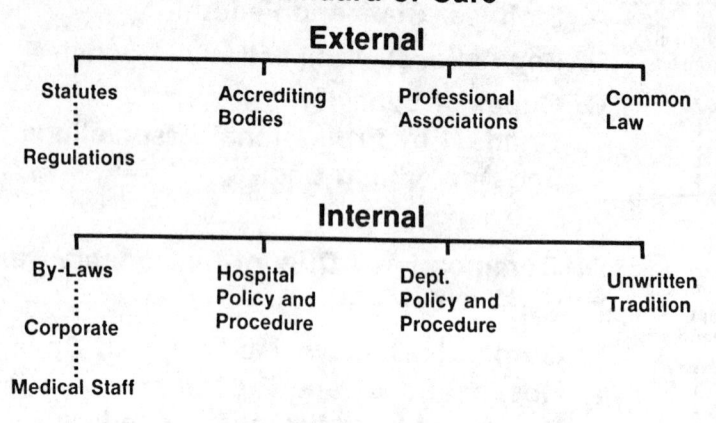

External

Statutes	Accrediting Bodies	Professional Associations	Common Law
Regulations			

Internal

By-Laws	Hospital Policy and Procedure	Dept. Policy and Procedure	Unwritten Tradition
Corporate			
Medical Staff			

B. Breach of Standard

Testimony

Medical	Non-Medical

Documentation

Medical Record	Ancillary Record

C. Proximate Cause

D. Damages

Testimony   Records

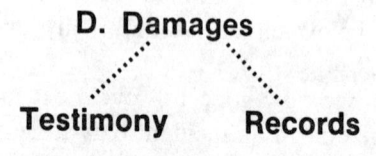

FIGURE 5–6. Integration of Various Standards of Care into a Plaintiff's Case

© copyright Cynthia M. Maleski, J.D., 1980

supervisor in the organizational structure and his or her relationship to the legal standard of care as derived from external and internal sources.

What is the managerial nurse's role in regard to departmental and institutional policies and procedures? Both departmental and institutional policies and procedures can be subpoenaed to show what the standard of care is for a particular institution or department. Policies and procedures, therefore, must reflect current practice. They must also be enforceable, and they must be practical and clearly written so that nursing personnel can apply them appropriately and efficiently. All staff, of course, must be made aware of the standards. And, finally, the policies and procedures must be regularly updated. This is not only a requirement of the various accrediting bodies such as the Joint Commission of Accreditation of Hospitals, but it also ensures that the policies and procedures reflect current trends.

What factors should a nursing supervisor consider in assigning a nurse to a particular unit or patient? It is the primary responsibility of the managerial nurse or nursing supervisor to assign to units personnel who are able to act competently within those units, and he or she can be held independently liable if assignment is done incorrectly. If externally imposed standards require that a nurse have certain skills and training before being assigned to a particular unit on a permanent basis, the supervisor must be sure that requirement is met. If the supervisor is assigning a nurse temporarily, he or she must inform the nurse that he or she can request help from more expert personnel for specific tasks and for the use of specialized equipment. Moreover, if a supervisor is informed by a staff nurse in a specialized unit that he or she does not know how to perform a necessary task, the supervisor is responsible for getting other personnel to perform that task.

Case law, however, does not tend to hold a supervisor liable if he or she assigns a task to an appropriately trained staff nurse who then proves incompetent to perform that task because the supervisor would not be expected to know about the nurse's incompetence. In *Bowers v. Olch* [121 Cal. App.2d 108, 260 P.2d 996 (1953)], the supervising nurse was not held liable for a surgical needle left in the abdomen of a patient because she had assigned two theoretically competent nurses to assist in the operating room.

In conclusion, we can only reiterate that a nurse needs to ask questions about job descriptions, hospital policies, scope of responsibilities, and expected competencies of personnel. Blind acceptance of rules and failure to think independently may endear nurses to those who like them to be submissive and subservient, but these tendencies will not help nurses to grow professionally, nor will they protect them in a court of law. Most important, they will not insure that the patient or client will receive the best possible nursing care.

6
Liability for Actions of Third Parties

Introduction

In recent years, increasing attention has been focused on the many people employed in health care facilities who have patient contact but are not employed directly by the health care agency or institution. Patients usually assume that anyone involved with their care has been screened by the health care provider. Moreover, they have a reasonable right to assume that these individuals are competent in their fields of health specialization.

Traditionally, there have been no clear delineations of the roles and responsibilities of the third-party health care workers. In recent years, however, the JCAH has become involved in this area and has identified some basic guidelines for hospitals to follow.

Private Employer Nurses

The private duty nurse employed by the patient, and the private employment agency nurse who provides additional care personnel to the institutions, are examples of third-party outside workers who are directly involved with patient care. Although permanent staff nurses frequently assist by answering questions and providing other support services to these nurses, it is unreasonable to expect them to assume total responsibility for supervising these personnel from outside agencies. The obligations that the staff nurses do have will be discussed throughout this section.

Although the private duty nurse is employed by the patient or his or her family, the private duty nurse must function within the established standards of the institution. He or she must report any changes in the patient's condition, the need for medical evaluation, the patient's daily progress or lack of progress, and other relevant conditions to the charge nurse. Like any other nurse, the private duty nurse has the obligation to perform only those nursing measures for which he or she feels competent and to seek assistance for other measures when necessary. This can place an especially troublesome burden on the nursing staff and the head nurse. When a private duty nurse or private agency nurse is unfamiliar with many nursing techniques, technical equipment, and policies, he or she is apt to seek assistance continually from nurses who already have a full load of their own.

Third-party nurses must therefore be evaluated periodically, as must other employees. The agency that provides a temporary nurse or private duty nurse will have its own designated mechanism for evaluation, but this mechanism should be acceptable to the hospital, which, under the ostensible agency doctrine, has the final responsibility for any practitioner who provides services to its patients and clients. If the staff nurse has any reason to question the competence of the third-party nurse, observations in this regard must be documented and communicated to the supervisor as they would be for any other employee (see Chapter 3).

There should be ongoing communication between the institution and the agency that handles the placement of third-party nurses. Institutions usually have some form of agreement that outlines the conditions under which these nurses can function, and these agreements can be reviewed annually or as circumstances demand.

The numbers of third-party nurses employed by private agencies and hired by hospitals to expand their staffs have increased. They work in acute, chronic, community-based, and other health care facilities. We realize that full-time staff nurses sometimes resent these temporary employees, but it is not our purpose to address the pros and cons of their use. We offer general guidelines, leaving it up to the institution to establish the specific rules under which they will operate. Any agreement or contract with third-party employees must be carefully discussed, reviewed, and modified as necessary.

The institution can also evaluate the performance of staff expanders, but a preliminary evaluation should be made by the agency before these individuals are sent to work in institutions. Many of the major agencies have developed evaluative techniques to determine competence. Many also have continuing education programs and urge individual nurses to update their skills as needed. Agencies also make periodic visits to the health care facilities employing their temporary nurses.

Any evaluation tool must be based on objective criteria and related to the standards of performance specified in the job description for which the nurse is being hired.

Until an institution has a measure of specific and specialized competencies of the nurse, his or her assignment should be limited to units that are supervised at all times by experienced staff nurses. The temporary nurse should not be assigned responsibilities beyond his or her level of competence.

Nursing Students

The JCAH "Standards for Nursing Services" require a written agreement to be in effect whenever clinical facilities are offered for the education of nursing students (JCAH, 1981, p. 116). This agreement between the institution (or health care agency) offering the clinical facilities and the school of nursing must define the respective roles and responsibilities of the institution and the school.

In addition to defining the educational program, the basic agreement between the clinical facility and the school can accurately and concisely define the duties of each institution in the program. The following are some items that such an agreement might contain:

1. the curriculum of the program and a statement of where the responsibility lies for the curriculum itself and for the instruction to students;
2. a clear description of which responsibilities for student supervision belong to faculty instructors and which belong to the health care facility staff;
3. a list of requirements for evidence of licensure, and a description of liability insurance coverage for faculty instructors and students;
4. health examination requirements for students and/or faculty instructors;
5. a description of the mechanisms to be used for evaluation of student performance, for the release of information about a student, and a statement of whether the health care facility is to become involved in these areas.

After such a document is drawn up, the head nurse on the unit and the faculty instructor must be made aware of its existence and its terms. The terms in such an agreement may sometimes act as guidelines for assessing accountability in ambiguous situations.

Questions and Answers

What sources outline the status and scope of responsibility permitted to third-party employees? Although many individuals acting within a hospital or institutional setting are not directly employed by the institution, it is the institution's responsibility to monitor their acts and status. This group can include individuals employed by physicians working in the institution, students in various programs, private duty nurses working in the institution, and many other persons employed by outside agencies, such as private health care agencies.

Many sources will inform a nurse who these individuals are and what their scope of responsibility is. For example, most state rules and regulations and the JCAH require affiliated training facilities and health care institutions to draw up an agreement that specifies their exact respective responsibilities. Staff nurses, especially head nurses, should be familiar with that agreement, especially as it pertains to responsibility toward student trainees.

In other cases, such as when an individual is employed by an outside contractor or physician, institutions often have contracts with both the physician and the third-party employee in order to determine scope of function. Job descriptions or checklists of privileges are often included in that contract. In addition, temporary nurses who were hired to work in a nursing department but are employed by a temporary service or a private duty registry should be listed as such in the nursing department so that they can be properly identified. They should also wear a tag showing their status and name so that staff personnel working on the units will know that they are authorized to act in some capacity on the unit.

What is a staff nurse's legal responsibility regarding private duty nurses or temporary nursing staff working on the unit? Staff nurses do not ordinarily have a legal responsibility for the private duty nurse or temporary nursing staff working in a unit. However, a staff nurse who is responsible to the same patient attended by a third-party nurse has an independent duty to ensure and monitor that patient's care. In relation to the nursing assessment process, the staff nurse is also responsible for halting a procedure in question or for otherwise intervening to protect the patient in an extreme emergency when negligence or an obviously wrongful act by another health care professional may cause serious harm to the patient. If the situation is not an emergency, the staff nurse is responsible for reporting his or her observations to the supervisor.

This question is often asked by staff nurses who work with private duty nurses, and even though we could find no cases involving nurses, cases do exist in which one physician has been held responsible for another's negligence after he had observed it but failed to fulfill his duty to take action [Conrad v. Lakewood General Hospital, 410 P.2d 785, 10 A.L.R.3d 1 (1966)].

What is the staff nurse's responsibility regarding nursing students who work on the unit? When a nursing student is found negligent, the faculty member, the staff nurse, and the head nurse from the institution can be brought into the lawsuit. The vicarious responsibility of instructors and of institutions, agencies, and their staffs for the actions of health care students engaged in clinical learning is still a changing area of the law. It is practical, however, for the staff nurse to know what his or her responsibility is for the placement and observation of nursing students within the unit. Does the instructor have the primary responsibility, or does the nurse? If the nurse is primarily responsible for instructing and observing students, the nurse could have a legal responsibility for placing students at the proper level of clinical instruction. In most instances, however, the faculty member has this responsibility. Nevertheless, the staff nurse could be held responsible if he or she knows, or should know from facts brought to his or her attention, that the student is not competent to perform certain tasks for a particular patient, especially if that patient is assigned to that staff nurse. Thus, if a student performs tasks that should be performed only by a licensed and experienced nurse, and does so with the staff nurse's knowledge, the nurse might be guilty of a breach of duty. Note that since case law is ambiguous in this area, this argument is tenable, and could be made by a patient's lawyer if harm occurs to the patient because of student action.

In what ways is a faculty member in a nursing school responsible for the actions of the nursing students under his or her clinical instruction? The nursing student's supervisor, whether he or she is the formally designated faculty member or the nurse in charge of the unit on which the student is working, can be held personally liable for harm resulting from a student's negligent performance, if the negligence occurs because the student is not yet competent to perform the assigned task according to the standard of competent professional nurses. In such a situation, the supervisor can be found to have breached the standard of competent nursing practice applicable to a supervisor (Warren, 1978, pp. 77–78). Thus, if an instructor knowingly or carelessly assigns a task beyond a student's capabilities, the instructor can be held liable for professional negligence if harm befalls the patient.

Can a nursing student be sued? If a patient suffers harm as a direct result of a nursing student's action, the student can be held personally liable. The hospital can also be held liable for the harm under the ostensible authority doctrine of agency law because a nursing student serving at the hospital on a patient care unit can be perceived by the patient as an employee of the hospital. The student is considered an ostensible or apparent employee even if he or she is from an affiliated school and not from the hospital's own school of nursing. In acting in the unit, the nursing student is held to the standard of a competent professional nurse in the performance of nursing duties. The reason for this seems to be that the courts feel it is unfair to deprive patients of the opportunity to recover damages for injury simply because nursing care was provided by a nursing student instead of a graduate professional nurse.

What should a staff nurse do if she or he observes a member of the health care team performing what is considered a clinically incorrect action? The nursing assessment process calls for a nurse to intervene immediately when he or she observes negligence by any other health care personnel that may cause serious harm to a patient. However, if the nurse feels the practice is clinically incorrect but is not causing immediate harm to the patient, he or she should report observations to the supervisor, whether the concern involves a student, another staff employee (nursing or otherwise), or a third-party employee. If the supervisor does not act within a reasonable period of time, the staff nurse should again submit any observations to the supervisor, this time in writing, objectively and with accurate dates and times of occurrences. This written report should not draw conclusions or express personal opinion. The staff nurse should keep a copy of the written memorandum for his or her own file.

Is it possible for a staff nurse to be responsible for any actions of a volunteer worker? Although it is currently not the practice of most health care institutions to permit volunteers to have direct patient contact, there may be circumstances in which the staff nurse can help to minimize the chances of the institution's or the staff's being responsible for a volunteer's actions. For example, if it has become a common practice in an institution for volunteer workers to perform certain patient care tasks, the staff nurse could inform his or her supervisor since such a use of volunteers should be monitored by the hospital. Even in situations where volunteers are allowed to perform rudimentary tasks for patients, the institution could be held responsible for any harm coming to a patient as a result—for example, if a volunteer inadvertently spills hot coffee on a patient and the patient receives a burn. The staff nurse, even though he or she is not primarily responsible for a volunteer's conduct, could therefore be held accountable if the nurse has been informed that the volunteer had been involved in previous similar incidents.

In addition, the staff nurse should not ask a volunteer to help or aid in taking care of a patient. In the case of *Marcus v. Frankford Hospital* [283 A.2d 69 Pa. (1971)], a fourteen-year-old volunteer, known as a candystriper, was asked by a staff nurse to hold a senile, incontinent patient while the nurse cleaned him. The young girl was not accustomed to such a situation and fainted, falling against an oxygen cylinder and breaking her nose. The volunteer sued the hospital, claiming that the nurse should have known better than to expose a young volunteer to the task of helping with such a patient.

Can a nursing student legally be directed by a staff nurse to perform a nursing measure that requires a physician order that has not yet been written if the staff nurse tells the student that the nurse will be responsible? The answer to this question may seem obvious, but a number of nursing students have informed us that this practice occurs. Because the nursing student is held to the standard of a professional nurse when he or she is operating in a patient care setting, the student must not perform a task that requires a physician order unless the physician order has been properly written down or (if the educational institution permits students to take verbal orders) verbally transmitted by the physician.

What documents or evidence can be used in a lawsuit to show that a student has reached a certain specific level of competence in performing a certain task? When a nursing student, a faculty member, and an institution are sued because of a student action, the first question that arises is whether the student was competent to perform the task at issue. A primary defense on the part of the institution, the faculty member, and the school of nursing is that the student was indeed performing at a proper level of competence before undertaking certain tasks. In attempting to prove this defense, a number of items could be brought into the case, such as the course objectives and the content and how far into the course the student had progressed at the time of the occurrence. Also of paramount importance would be the instructor's testimony and the opinion of an impartial instructor as to the expectable competence of a student at that particular point of education.

Should a nursing student who also is employed as a nursing assistant be permitted to perform tasks beyond those allowed a nonstudent nursing assistant in a particular institution? Most nursing students work on weekends or in the evenings as nursing assistants. Even though they may be allowed to perform duties usually ascribed professional nurses as students under clinical instruction, they should not be allowed to perform any tasks except those allowed nonstudent nursing assistants working in a part-time capacity. The nursing student must therefore refer to the job description for a nursing assistant to find out what he or she is allowed to do when working in that position.

Epilogue

In 1948, Esther Lucile Brown observed:

> Nurses have suffered frustration from the system of institutionalism within which they have worked and lived, and from insufficient sympathetic understanding by other health services and the public, as well as from their own inadequacies. This frustration has produced lack of self-confidence, which has transmitted itself to society. The public, in turn, has responded by continual disinterest or by sharp criticism. Thus a vicious cycle has been institutionalized and perpetualized. [Brown, p. 198]

It has been said by nurses that "we have met the enemy and they are us."

The seminars we present have emphasized to us that many nurses have overcome the apathy, the lack of self-confidence, and the feelings of inadequacies that have held them back. Many more want to, but have not yet fully achieved their goal. We have found cases in which the nurse who wishes to be accountable, assertive, and self-confident has been viewed with suspicion and distrust as a troublemaker and has been not-so-subtly intimidated by peers and supervisors. The camaraderie needed to create a cohesive and viable group that supports and encourages professional accountability has not always been sufficient to make a significant impact.

When we encourage nurses to be risk takers, we want them to do so only when the risk is not to the safety and welfare of the patient or client. What we advocate is the risk entailed in speaking up for one's own convictions, in defending one's position, and in asking questions.

When we first met to plan our initial seminar, Cynthia Maleski commented that of all the health professionals she had observed, nurses were the most docile, the ones who questioned the least. How often does one hear a nurse say, "But I am only a nurse—what can I do?" Many nurses are still being led and are still submitting to the image of the second- or third-rate member of the health team.

Today a nurse has many options for changing this image. Practice acts are still evolving, and educational programs have introduced ways to help the nurse become an agent for positive change. Patient care and the commitment to patient welfare have consistently characterized most nurses. The challenge now is to combine all the forces—legal, educational, political, and social—to allow nurses to render the best possible care to any and all who need nursing in its broadest definition.

Our purpose in writing this book has been to present some basic guidelines to give dedicated nurses a firmer ground on which to achieve and base accountability, and to introduce the sources of guidance nurses can consult when they meet clinical situations that can increase the risk of professional error and liability.

Our final word is that fear of malpractice will not be the primary motive for nurses to develop legal awareness and clinical competence. The primary motives will be the same as those which have inspired professional nursing since the beginning: caring; compassion and comfort; and the safety and welfare of patients, their families, and significant others.

Appendixes

Appendix A
Responsibilities of the Registered Nurse
49.§21.11. Department of State
Ch. 21. State Board of Nurse Examiners 49§21.11

Throughout the book, we have urged the nurse to be aware of the nurse practice act, rules, regulations, and joint statements because she is held accountable for this knowledge. We have included selected samples from the Commonwealth of Pennsylvania. Each nurse should know where this material is filed in the facility where she is employed. Individual copies are generally available, for a fee, through the state nurses associations.

§21.11. General functions.

(a) The registered nurse assesses human responses and plans, implements and evaluates nursing care for individuals or families for whom the nurse is responsible. In carrying out this responsibility, the nurse performs all the following functions:

(1) Collects complete and ongoing data to determine nursing care needs.
(2) Analyzes the health status of the individuals and families and compares the data with the norm when possible in determining nursing care needs.
(3) Identifies goals and plans for nursing care.
(4) Carries out nursing care actions which promote, maintain, and restore the well-being of individuals.
(5) Involves individuals and their families in their health promotion, maintenance, and restoration.
(6) Evaluates the effectiveness of the quality of nursing care provided.
(b) The registered nurse is fully responsible for all actions as a licensed nurse and is accountable to clients for the quality of care delivered.
(c) The registered nurse shall not engage in areas of highly specialized practice without adequate knowledge of and skills in the practice areas involved.
(d) The Board recognizes standards of practice and professional codes of behavior, as developed by appropriate nursing associations, as the criteria for assuring safe and effective practice.

§21.12. Veni puncture; intravenous fluids.

Performing of veni puncture and administering and withdrawing intravenous fluids are functions regulated by this sections, and such functions shall not be performed unless all of the following are met:

(1) The procedure has been ordered in writing for the patient by a licensed doctor of the healing arts.
(2) The nurse who performs veni punctures has had instruction and supervised practice in performing veni punctures.
(3) The nurse who administers parenteral fluids, drugs, or blood has had instruction and supervised practice in administering parenteral fluids, blood, or medications into the vein.
(4) A list of medications which may be administered by the nurse is established and maintained by a committee of physicians, pharmacists, and nurses from the employing agency or the agency within whose jurisdiction the procedure is being performed if no employing agency is involved.

Appendix A

  (5) The intravenous fluid or medication to be administered is the fluid or medication specified in the written order.
  (6) The blood is identified as the blood ordered for the patient.
  (7) An accurate record is made concerning the following:
   (i) The time of the injection.
   (ii) The medication or fluid injected.
   (iii) The amount of medication or fluid injected.
   (iv) Any reactions to the fluid.

§21.13. Resuscitation and respiration.

External cardiac resuscitation and artificial respiration, mouth-to-mouth, are procedures regulated by this section, and such functions shall not be performed unless both of the following provisions are met:

  (1) External cardiac resuscitation and artificial respiration, mouth-to-mouth, shall only be performed by a nurse on an individual when respiration or pulse, or both, cease unexpectedly.
  (2) A nurse shall not perform external cardic resuscitation and artificial respiration, mouth-to-mouth, unless the nurse has had instruction and supervised practice in performing the procedures.

§21.14. Administration of drugs.

The administration to a patient of a drug ordered for that patient by a licensed doctor of the healing arts in the dosage prescribed is a procedure regulated by this section, and such function shall not be performed except that a licensed registered nurse, responsible for administering a drug, may supervise a person other than a licensed registered nurse responsible for administering a drug, such as a nursing student in an approved program or a graduate nurse as provided for in Section 4(4) of the act (63 P.S. §214(4)), in the administration of the drug. As used in this section, supervision shall mean that the registered nurse is physically present in the area or unit where the student or unlicensed graduate is practicing. This definition of supervision is not intended to limit in any way the practice of practical nursing as defined in the act.

§21.15. Monitoring, defibrillating, and resuscitating.*

  *Source: The provisions of this §21.15 amended Nov. 19, 1970, 1 Pa.B.804.

The use of monitoring, defibrillating, or resuscitating equipment, or any combination of the three, hereinafter called "therapy," is a proper function of a registered nurse and is a function regulated by this section; such function shall not be performed unless all of the following provisions are met:

(1) The employer, through written policy, has agreed that the registered nurse may administer such therapy.
(2) A committee of licensed physicians and nurses within the employing agency has established written criteria prescribing when such therapy shall be administered by a registered nurse either in the presence or absence of the attending physician.
(3) The techniques for administering such therapy have been established by a committee of licensed physicians and registered nurses within the employing agency.
(4) The registered nurse has had instruction and supervised practice in administering such therapy.
(5) The registered nurse has demonstrated competency in administering such therapy to the satisfaction of the employer.
(6) The registered nurse shall have employed the prescribed techniques in administering such therapy in accordance with the established criteria.

§21.16. Immunizations.

(a) Immunization and skin testing is a proper function of a registered nurse and is a function regulated by this section, and such function shall not be performed unless all of the following conditions are met:
(1) A written order has been issued by a licensed physician. Such order may be a standing order applicable to individuals or groups.
(2) The policies and procedures under which the registered nurse may administer immunizing agents and do skin testing have been established by a committee representing the nurses, the physicians, and the administration of the agency or institution. Such written policies and procedures must be available to the nurse. The committee should also perform the following functions:

Appendix A

      (i) Identify the immunizing and skin testing agents which the nurse may administer.
     (ii) Determine the contraindications for the administration of specific immunizing and skin testing agents.
    (iii) Outline medical principles governing the treatment of possible anaphylactic reactions.
    (iv) Establish instruction and supervised practice required to insure competency in administering immunizing and skin testing agents.
  (b) Following skin testing, the size of the induration or its absence may be observed and recorded by the properly instructed registered nurse.

§21.17. Anesthesia.

The administration of anesthesia is a proper function of a registered nurse and is a function regulated by this section; such function shall not be performed unless all of the following provisions are met:

(1) The registered nurse has successfully completed the educational program of a school for nurse anesthetists accredited by the American Association of Nurse Anesthetists.
(2) The registered nurse is certified as a Registered Nurse Anesthetist by the American Association of Nurse Anesthetists within one year following completion of the educational program.
(3) The registered nurse administers such anesthesia under the direction of and in the presence of a licensed physician or dentist.

Statement of the Administration of Intravenous Fluids

The Medical Society of the State of Pennsylvania, the Hospital Association of Pennsylvania, The Pennsylvania Osteopathic Association, the Pennsylvania League for Nursing, and the Pennsylvania Nurses Association recognize that it is proper practice and sound procedure for a licensed professional nurse to administer fluids intravenously and/or withdraw venous blood under the following conditions, all of which must be met in each situation:

1. The nurse who performs either procedure has had proper instruction and practice.

2. The procedure has been ordered for the specific patient by a licensed doctor of medicine or osteopathy.
3. In hospitals where nurses perform these procedures, a joint committee representing administration, medical or osteopathic staff, and the department of nursing shall formally prescribe, in writing, the conditions under which and the manner in which these procedures shall be performed by nurses. These written statements of policies are to be published and distributed to the total medical and nursing staff. It is the jurisdiction of this joint committee to:
   a. List in writing the types of fluids and medications that nurses may administer intravenously.
   b. Determine the proper instruction and practice necessary for the performance of these procedures.
   c. Establish and maintain a roster of those nurses who have had proper instruction and practice in these instructions.
   d. Establish in-service programs for those nurses who have not had proper instruction and practice in these procedures.
   e. Provide facilities to disseminate current information.
4. In all other situations, outside the jurisdiction of hospitals, the administration of intravenous fluids and/or the withdrawal of venous blood may be performed by a professional nurse who has had proper instruction and practice in these techniques when so authorized by responsible medical authority.

Appendix B
Joint Statement on Inhalation Therapy

- Pennsylvania Nurses Association
- Hospital Association of Pennsylvania
- Pennsylvania Department of Health
- Pennsylvania Department of Public Welfare
- Pennsylvania League for Nursing
- Pennsylvania Medical Society
- State Board of Nurse Examiners
- Pennsylvania Osteopathic Association

It is recognized by the above that inhalation therapy programs are fast becoming an important part of total patient care. The overall supervision and the ultimate responsibility for the patient's plan of medical care is that of the attending physician. Therefore, it is the physician who prescribes inhalation therapy. The registered nurse has the responsibility for assessing the nursing needs of patients, for planning and giving nursing care, and for coordinating all aspects of patient care. Therefore, the registered nurse must know the principles of respiratory therapy and techniques using the equipment.

When there is an inhalation therapy department in the employing agency, the registered nurse recognizes the inhalation therapist as one who is well trained in all aspects of inhalation therapy and experienced in its clinical applications, and the nurse communicates and cooperates with the inhalation therapist in planning and coordinating therapy for patients.

If there is not an inhalation therapy department, the registered nurse may assume responsibility for administering inhalation therapy as ordered by the physician, provided the following conditions are met:

1. The hospital or employing agency has established through written policy that registered nurses may administer inhalation therapy.
2. The techniques for using the equipment have been established by a committee of the physicians and nurses within the agency or institution.
3. The registered nurse has had instructions and practice in using the equipment.
4. The registered nurse has demonstrated competency in performing these techniques to the satisfaction of the committee.

Appendix C
A Statement of Principle Regarding the Position of the Professional Nurse and the Pharmacist in the Handling of Drugs

The Pennsylvania Nurses Association and the Pennsylvania Pharmaceutical Association have been made aware by their members and by procedures which exist primarily in certain hospitals of the necessity to promulgate a joint statement of principle reiterating the status and responsibilities of the professional nurse and the pharmacist with regard to the handling of drugs.

According to The Professional Nursing Law (Section 2(1)), a person engages in the practice of professional nursing, within the meaning of the law, who performs any professional services requiring the application of the principles of the biological sciences, prevention of disease or in the conservation of health.

Likewise, according to The Professional Nursing Law (Section 5 (2)), the curriculum of schools of nursing must provide the student with responsible supervision of a patient in carrying out the treatments and medications prescribed by a licensed physician.

Therefore, professional nurses are educated and subsequently duly licensed only to administer medications: administration is the giving of a unit dose of medication to a patient as a result of a physician's order. Administration affects only one patient.

Conversely, according to the Pharmacy Act (Section 2 (11)), the practice of pharmacy means the practice of that profession concerned with the art and sciences of preparing, compounding, and dispensing of drugs and devices, whether dispensed on the prescription of a medical practitioner or legally dispensed or sold directly to the ultimate consumer, and includes the proper and safe storage and distribution of drugs, the maintenance of proper records, therefore, and the responsibility of relating information as required concerning such drugs and the medicines and their therapeutic values and uses in the treatment and prevention of disease.

The Pharmacist is educated and duly licensed to dispense medications. Dispensing is defined as the issuing of one or more doses in a suitable container, such container being properly labeled by the dispenser as to contents and directions for use. Dispensing affects one or many patients. Thus, a pharmacist, whether in a hospital or elsewhere, has the sole responsibility for dispensing medication either for individual use or as floor stock.

These existing laws and regulations, as well as the traditions and ethics of the professions, exist for the purpose of protecting public health and welfare. Their practical effect is in substance: that nurses are licensed only to administer medications—not to dispense drugs; pharmacists are licensed to dispense medications for the use of others—not to administer drugs. Therefore, nurses, as well as all other persons not properly qualified, should not be required to, nor be permitted to, dispense drugs or perform other pharmaceutical functions.

References:

1. The Professional Nursing Law, Act of May 22, 1951, P.L. 317.
2. The Pharmacy Act, Act of September 27, 1961, P.L. 1700.
3. R. Kenna, "Drugs at All Hours: Solving the Problem of 24-Hour Pharmacy Service," *Hospitals,* Vol. 37, No. 12 (June 16, 1963), pp. 77–78.

Appendix D
The Professional Nursing Law in Pennsylvania: An Act

Relating to the practice of professional nursing; providing for the licensing of nurses and for the revocation and suspension of such licenses, subject to appeal, and for their reinstatement; providing for the renewal of such licenses; regulating nursing in general; prescribing penalties and repealing certain laws.

The General Assembly of the Commonwealth of Pennsylvania hereby enacts as follows:

Section 1. This act shall be known and may be cited as "The Professional Law."

Section 2. When used in this act, the following words and phrases shall have the following meanings unless the context provides otherwise:

(1) The "Practice of Professional Nursing" means diagnosing and treating human responses to actual or potential health problems through such services as case-finding, health teaching, health counseling, and provision of care supportive to or restorative of life and well-being, and executing medical regimens as prescribed by a licensed physician or dentist. The foregoing shall not be deemed to include acts of medical diagnosis or prescription of medical, therapeutic or corrective measures, except as may be authorized by

rules and regulations jointly promulgated by the State Board of Medical Education and Licensure and the Board, which rules and regulations shall be implemented by the Board.
(2) "Board" means the State Board of Nurse Examiners.
(3) "Approved" means approved by the State Board of Nurse Examiners.
(4) "Diagnosing" means that identification of and discrimination between physical and psychosocial signs and symptoms essential to effective execution and management of the nursing regimen.
(5) "Treating" means selection and performance of those therapeutic measures essential to the effective execution and management of the nursing regimen, and execution of the prescribed medical regimen.
(6) "Human responses" means those signs, symptoms and processes which denote the individual's interaction with an actual or potential health problem.

Section 2.1. The Board shall have the right and duty to establish rules and regulations for the practice of professional nursing and the administration of this act. Copies of such rules and regulations shall be available for distribution to the public.

Section 3. Any person who holds a license to practice professional nursing in this Commonwealth, or who is maintained on inactive status in accordance with Section 11 of this act, shall have the right to use the title "registered nurse" and the abbreviation "R.N." No other person shall engage in the practice of professional nursing or use the title "registered nurse" or the abbreviation "R.N." to indicate that the person using the same is a registered nurse. No person shall sell or fraudulently obtain or fraudulently furnish any nursing diploma, license, record, or registration or aid or abet therein.

Section 4. This act confers no authority to practice dentistry, podiatry, optometry, chiropractic medicine or surgery, nor does it prohibit:
(1) Home care of the sick by friends, domestic servants, nursemaids, companions, or household aides of any type, so long

as such persons do not represent or hold themselves out to be licensed nurses, licensed registered nurses, or registered nurses; or use in connection with their names, any designation tending to imply that they are licensed to practice under the provisions of this act nor services rendered by any physicians, osteopaths, dentists or chiropractors, podiatrists, optometrists, or any person licensed pursuant to the act of March 2, 1956 (P.L. 1211 No. 376), known as the "Practical Nurse Law."

(2) Care of the sick, with or without compensation or personal profit, when done solely in connection with the practice of the religious tenets of any church by adherents thereof.

(3) The practice of professional nursing by a person temporarily in this Commonwealth licensed by another state, territory or possession of the United States or a foreign country, in compliance with an engagement made outside of this Commonwealth, which engagement requires that such person accompany and care for a patient while temporarily in this Commonwealth: provided, however, that said engagement shall not be of more than six (6) months' duration.

(4) The practice of professional nursing by a graduate of an approved program of professional nursing in Pennsylvania or any other state, working under qualified supervision, during a period not to exceed one (1) year between completion of his or her program and notification of the results of a licensing examination taken by such person, and during such additional period as the Board may in each case especially permit.

(5) The practice of professional nursing by a person who holds a current license or other evidence of the right to practice professional nursing, as that term is defined in this act, issued by any other state, territory or possession of the United States or the Dominion of Canada, during the period that an application filed by such person for licensure in Pennsylvania is pending before the Board, but not for a period of more than one (1) year.

(6) The practice of professional nursing, within the definition of this act, by any person when such person is engaged in the practice of nursing as an employee of the United States.

Section 5.

(a) The Board shall, once every year and at such other times and under such conditions as shall be provided by its regulations, examine all eligible applicants for licensure; and shall, subject to the provisions of Section 6 of this act, issue a license to each person passing said examination to the satisfaction of the Board.

(b) The Board may admit to examination any person who has satisfactorily completed an approved nursing education program for the preparation of registered professional nurses in Pennsylvania or such a program in any other state, territory or possession of the United States, considered by the Board to be equivalent to that required in this Commonwealth at the time such program was completed, and who meets the requirements of character and preliminary education.

(c) The Board may admit to examination any person who has satisfactorily completed a nursing education program for the preparation of registered professional nurses in a country or territory not mentioned above who has been licensed, registered, or duly recognized there as a professional nurse provided such a program is considered by the Board to be equal to that required in this Commonwealth at the time such program was completed and who meets the requirements of character and preliminary education.

Section 6. No application for licensure as a registered nurse shall be considered unless accompanied by a fee of ten dollars ($10). Every applicant, to be eligible for examination for licensure as a registered nurse, shall furnish evidence satisfactory to the Board that he or she is of good moral character, has completed work equal to a standard high school course as evaluated by the Board, and has satisfactorily completed an approved program of professional nursing.

Section 6.1. The Board shall establish standards for operation and approval of nursing education programs for the preparation of registered professional nurses and for the carrying out of the rights given to the Board under this act. Programs for the preparation of registered professional nurses shall be established or conducted only with the approval of the Board. The Board shall

Appendix D

establish standards and approve organized programs of study offered to foreign graduate nurses in the United States on non-immigration status who are studying in this Commonwealth. Initial approval shall be followed by at least annual survey and review of the program to assure maintenance of acceptable standards. Such programs shall be conducted only with approval of the Board. Each hospital maintaining an exchange visitor educational program for foreign graduate nurses shall pay a fee as established by the Board. Such fee shall be related to the actual costs incurred by the Board in rendering services in connection with such programs.

Section 6.2. The Board shall annually prepare and make available for public distribution a list of all programs approved and classified by it. Any student who shall be enrolled in any school which shall be removed from the approved list shall be given credit toward the satisfaction of the Board's requirements for examination for such of the requirements of the Board which any said student shall satisfactorily complete prior to the removal of said school from the approved list, and said student shall upon the satisfactory completion of the remainder of said requirements in any approved school be eligible for examination for licensure. The Board may withhold or remove any school from the approved list if the school fails to meet and maintain minimum standards, as established by regulation of the Board of education, curriculum, administration, qualifications of the faculty, organization and functions of the faculty, staff and facilities.

Section 7. The Board may issue a license without examination to a graduate of a school of nursing who has completed a course of study in nursing considered by the Board to be equivalent to that required in this State at the time such course was completed, and who is registered or licensed by examination in any other state or territory of the United States or the Dominion of Canada, and who has met all the foregoing requirements as to character and preliminary education.

Section 8. The Board shall issue to each person who meets the licensure requirements of this act, a certificate setting forth that such person is licensed to engage in the practice of professional nursing and entitled to use the title "registered nurse" and the letters "R.N."

Section 9 & Section 10. Repealed (content now contained in Sections 2.1 and 6.2 respectively).

Section 11.

(a) Licenses issued pursuant to this act shall expire on the thirty-first day of October of each biennium, or on such other biennial expiration date as may be established by regulation of the Board. Application for renewal of a license shall biennially be forwarded to each registrant holding a current license prior to the expiration date of the current renewal biennium. The application form may be completed and returned to the Board, accompanied by the required fee of four dollars ($4); upon approval of each application, the applicant shall receive a renewal of license.

(b) Any registrant licensed under this act may request an application for inactive status. The application form may be completed and returned to the Board. Upon receipt of each application, the application shall be maintained on inactive status without fee and shall be entitled to apply at any time and to receive a current license by filing a renewal application as in subsection (a) hereof.

Section 12. Repealed (content now contained in Section 3).

Section 13. Any person, or the responsible officers or employees of any corporation, copartnership, institution or association violating any of the provisions of this act, shall, upon summary conviction thereof, be sentenced to pay a fine of three hundred dollars ($300); and in default of the payment of such fine and costs, to undergo imprisonment for a period of ninety (90) days, unless nonpayment of said fine is shown by affidavit made by the defendant to the court, to be the result of the defendant's indigency.

Section 14. The Board may suspend or revoke any license in any case where the Board shall find that:

Appendix D

(1) The licensee is on repeated occasions negligent or incompetent in the practice of professional nursing.
(2) The licensee is unable to practice professional nursing with reasonable skill and safety to patients by reason of mental or physical illness or condition or physiological and psychological dependence upon alcohol, hallucinogenic or narcotic drugs or other drugs which tend to impair judgment or coordination, so long as such dependence shall continue. In enforcing this clause (2), the Board shall, upon probable cause, have authority to compel a licensee to submit to a mental or physical examination as designated by it. After notice, hearing, adjudication and appeal as provided for in Section 15, failure of a licensee to submit to such examination when directed shall constitute an admission of the allegations against him or her unless failure is due to circumstances beyond his or her control, consequent upon which a default and final order may be entered without the taking of testimony or presentation of evidence. A licensee affected under this paragraph shall at reasonable intervals be afforded an opportunity to demonstrate that he or she can resume a competent practice or professional nursing with reasonable skill and safety to patients.
(3) The licensee has wilfully or repeatedly violated any of the provisions of this act or of the regulations of the Board.
(4) The licensee has committed fraud or deceit in the practice of nursing, or in securing his or her admission to such practice.
(5) The licensee has been convicted, or has pleaded guilty, or entered a plea of *nolo contendere*, or has been found guilty by a judge or jury, or a felony in the courts of this Commonwealth or any other state, territory, or country.
(6) The licensee has his license suspended or revoked in another state, territory, or country.

Section 15. All suspensions and revocations shall be made only in accordance with the regulations of the Board, and only by majority vote of the members of the Board after a full and fair hearing before the Board. All actions of the Board shall be taken subject to the right of notice, hearing and adjudication, and the right of appeal therefrom, in accordance with the provisions of the Administrative Agency Law, approved the fourth day of June, one thousand nine hundred forty-five (Pamphlet Laws 1388), or any amendment or reenactment thereof, relating to adjudication procedure. The Board, by majority action and in accordance with its regulations, may reissue any license which has been suspended or revoked.

Note: Act Number 69, P.L. 317, May 22, 1951, as amended by
Act Number 151, July 3, 1974
Act Number 118, P.L. 353, May 6, 1970
Act Number 73, P.L. 135, May 29, 1968
Act Number 689, P.L. 1888, December 17, 1959

Glossary

American Nurses' Association—the official professional nursing association in the United States.

Appellate Court—the court having jurisdiction of appeal and review.

Case law—the law of a particular subject as evidenced or formed by adjudged or decided cases in distinction to statutes and other sources of law.

Common law—is distinguished from law created by the enactment of legislatures. It comprises the body of those principles and rules of action that derive their authority solely from usages and customs of immemorial antiquity, or from judgments and decrees of the courts, recognizing, affirming, and enforcing such usages and customs.

Defendant—the person defending or denying; the party against whom relief or recovery is sought in an action or suit.

Discovery—the acquisition of notice or knowledge of given acts or facts.

Evidentiary—having the quality of evidence.

Indemnification—the action whereby one party compensates another for loss incurred by that second party.

JCAH—The Joint Commission for Accreditation of Hospitals, which annually publishes the *Accreditation Manual for Hospi-*

tals. This manual includes principles, standards, and interpretation of areas of health care.

Jurisdiction—the limits or territory within which authority may be exercised.

Ostensible agency doctrine—an implied or presumptive agency that exists where one, either intentionally or from want of ordinary care, induces another to believe that a third person is his or her agent or employee, though he or she never in fact employed that individual.

Plaintiff—a person who brings an action; the party who complains or sues in a personal action.

Res ipsa loquitur—"the thing speaks for itself"; a theory of law that states with proof that the person or thing causing the injury was in the defendant's exclusive control and that the accident is one that does not ordinarily happen in the absence of negligence.

Respondeat superior—"let the master answer"; this maxim means that a master is liable in certain cases for the wrongful acts of his or her servant, and an employer for those of his or her employee.

Risk management—an integrated program of protection of the institution's assets, including, but not limited to, risk identification, risk control, risk transfer, and risk minimization. A key element of an effective program is identification of problem areas by those who give clinical care and appropriate correction action to ameliorate problem situations.

Statutory law—that which is introduced or governed by statute or written law, as opposed to common law.

Tort—a private or civil wrong or injury; a wrong independent of contract.

References

Alexander, E. *Nursing Administration in the Hospital Health Care System.* St. Louis: Mosby, 1978.
American Hospital Association. *A Patient's Bill of Rights.* Chicago: American Hospital Association, 1972.
American Nurses' Association. *Code for Nurses with Interpretive Statements,* Kansas City, Mo.: ANA, 1978.
American Nurses' Association. *Standards of Nursing Practice.* Kansas City, Mo.: ANA, 1973.
Brown, E.L. *Nursing for the Future.* New York: Russell Sage Foundation, 1948.
Bullough, B. *The Law and the Expanding Nurse Role.* 2d ed. New York: Appleton-Century-Crofts, 1980.
Cazalas, M. W. *Nursing and the Law.* Germantown, Md.: Aspen Systems Corporation, 1978.
Corless, I. "Nursing Professionalization and Innovation" in *Current Perspectives in Nursing,* ed. B. Flynn & M. Miller. St. Louis: Mosby, 1980.
Creighton, H. "Law for the Nurse Supervisor," *Supervisor Nurse* (June 1980), pp. 61-62.
Duncanis, A. & A. Golen. *The Interdisciplinary Health Care Team.* Germantown, Md.: Aspen Systems Corporation, 1979.
Golen, A. & A. Duncanis. "Interdisciplinary Implications of the Ethical Standards of the Health Professions." Paper presented at the meeting of the Association of Schools of the Allied Health Professions, Dallas, Texas, November 1977.
Grunder, T. M. "On the Readability of Surgical Consent Forms," *New England Journal of Medicine* (April 17, 1980), pp. 900-902.

Joint Commission on Accreditation of Hospitals. *Accreditation Manual for Hospitals*. Chicago: JCAH, 1981.

Kelly, L. "Keeping Up with Your Legal Responsibilities," *Nursing '76*, Vol. 6 (March 1976), p. 83.

Manpower Analysis Branch, Bureau of Health Manpower. *A Report to the President and Congress on the Status of Health Profession's Personnel in the United States*. Washington, D.C.: Department of Health and Human Services, Department of Health, Education, and Welfare, August 1978.

McAllister, J. B. *Ethics with Special Application to the Medical and Nursing Professions*. 2d ed. Philadelphia: Saunders, 1955.

Orem, D. E. *Nursing Concepts of Practice*. New York: McGraw-Hill, 1971.

Perry, S. "Managing to Avoid Malpractice," *Journal of Nursing Administration*, Vol. 8 (August 1978), p. 44.

Recommendations of Privacy Protection Study Commission, Privacy Act of 1974. Washington, D.C., 1977.

Warren, G. *Problems in Hospital Law*. 3d ed. Germantown, Md.: Aspen Systems Corporation, 1978.

Willig, S. *The Nurses' Guide to the Law*. New York: McGraw-Hill, 1970.

Index

Abbreviations, 71
Abortion, consent of the spouse to, 22
Access to medical records, *see* Medical records
Affirmative action, duty of, 42
Alexander, E., 25, 29, 30
American Hospital Association (AHA), 27
   on right of informed consent, 7
   standards of nursing care of, 29–30
American Nurses Association (ANA)
   Code of Ethics, 82, 83
   on recordkeeping, 50
   standards of practice of, 28–30, 46–47
Anesthesia, informed consent before, 16
Assessment, documentation and, 70
Attorney's access to information in medical records, 63

Bill of rights, *see* Patient's bill of rights
Bowers v. Olch, 120
Breach of standard of care, 36
Brown, Esther Lucile, 131

Budgen v. Harbor View Hospital, 102
Bullough, B., 88

Causation, proximate, 36–37
Cazalas, M. W., 108
Chart(ing), 52, 53
   on consecutive lines, 68
   correcting errors in, 68
   cosignature on, 68–69
   dietary information in, 70
   reference to specific protocol in, 67
   signing one's name to a, 68
Chiropractors, orders prescribed by, 85
Citizens Hospital v. Schoulin, 98
Clinically incorrect actions, 127–128
Collins v. Westlake Community Hospital, 54
Community standards of practice, 40–41
Competence of nursing students, 129
Confidentiality of medical records, 56, 57
   right to, 107–108
Consent, *see* Informed consent
Cooper v. National Bearing Company, 87, 100, 106
Corless, I., 97

157

Cosignature on a patient's chart, 68–69
Creighton, H., 52

Damaged or lost belongings, 104–105
Damages, proof of, 37
Darling v. Charleston Community Memorial Hospital, 34–35, 101–102
Delaware, informed consent statute of, 5–6
Dentists, orders prescribed by, 85
Diagnosis
  independent liability for, 100
  medical versus nursing, 87–88
Dictation of physician orders, 105
Diets, documentation concerning, 70
Disciplinary problems, documentation of, 75–76
Disclosure
  to parents, of information that a minor patient does not wish revealed, 19
  by the physician to the patient, informed consent and, 2–4, 12
Documentation
  of disciplinary problems, 75–76
  of follow-up measures and evaluation, 53–54, 69
  general guidelines for correct, 65–66
  of general nursing care, 70–71
  of inadequate staffing, 74
  Joint Commission on Accreditation of Hospitals on, 51, 54–55, 58
  letters, symbols, and abbreviations in, 71
  liability and, 43, 54
  nursing assessment process and, 70
  of nutrition, 70
  of a refusal to follow physician orders, 86
  of suspected unprofessional conduct or incompetency of others, 72–74
  of tasks performed by others, 72
  See also Medical records; Recordkeeping
"Do not resuscitate" (DNR) order, 88–89
Ducanis, A., 82, 83

Emergency situations
  good Samaritan statutes and, 110
  informed consent and, 15
Employee records, 77–78
Engle v. Clarke, 54
Experimental procedures, informed consent to, 23

Factual translation, 103
Flow sheets, 67

Goff v. Doctor's General Hospital, 42
Golen, A., 82, 83
Good Samaritan statutes, 110
Grunder, T. M., 4

Health care teams, *see* Interdisciplinary practice issues
Hiatt v. Groce, 40
Hospitals, supervisory nurses's responsibilities and organizational structure of, 112–119

Implied consent, doctrine of, 2
Incompetence
  documentation of, 72–74
  in a health care professional other than a nurse, 95
  next-of-kin consent and determination of, 19
  nurse's role with regard to informed consent and, 20

Index

Independent functions of nurses, 96–97
Independent liability, 96–120
  for administration of an injection, 102
  for administration of medication, 101
  for assignment of nurses to particular units or patients, 119–120
  bases of suits besides professional liability, 103–104
  competence for assignment to a specialty unit and, 105–106
  departmental and institutional policies and procedures and, 119
  dictation of physician orders and, 105
  in different settings, 106–107
  of faculty member for the actions of nursing students, 126–127
  for the general safety of patients, 102–103
  good Samaritan statutes and, 110
  for identification of potential or actual problems by nursing supervisors, 111
  for intentional wrongs, 103–104
  for interpretation and execution of physician orders, 100–101
  liability insurance and, 109
  for lost or damaged belongings, 104–105
  of managerial or supervisory nurses, 110–120
  for monitoring patient's symptoms, 101–102
  for nursing diagnosis, 100
  of nursing students, 127
  patient's bill of rights and, 108–109
  patient's right to confidentiality and privacy and, 107–108
  privileged communication and, 107–108
  respondeat superior doctrine and, 99, 112–113
  responsibility as an employee of an institution and, 99–100
  situation and bases of, 98–100
  of staff nurses, 98–110
  of staff nurses regarding nursing students, 126, 128–129
  of staff nurses regarding private duty nurses or temporary nursing staff, 125–126
  tasks that carry the greatest legal risks, 100–103
  temporary assignments to a specialty unit and, 105
Informed consent, 1–24
  delegation of responsibility for obtaining, 3, 8–10
  development of doctrine of, 1–2
  disclosure by the physician to the patient and, 2–4, 12
  doubts of patient about previous consent, 13–14
  doubts of patient immediately before surgery, 14
  to emergency department procedures, 15–16
  emergency situations and, 15
  execution of a consent form, 13
  form for, 8–9
  general consent form, 2
  implied consent, 2
  incompetency and, 19, 20
  to inoculations, 22
  to investigational drugs or experimental procedures, 23
  language understandable to the patient required for, 4
  Mature Minor Rule and, 17
  mental health facility and, 21
  minors and, 16–19
  by next-of-kin, 19–21
  by nonparental caretakers, 18–19
  nurse as a witness to the signature on a consent form, 10

Informed consent (*continued*)
  by a nurse in a health care facility, for treatment of a minor, 18–19
  obligation for obtaining, 3–4, 8
  oral, 9
  patient's bill of rights as basis for rules and regulations on, 6–7
  procedures for which there is a requirement of, 3
  reason for requirement of, 3
  recording the time of signing, 11
  refusal of treatment and, 23–24
  of the spouse, 21–22
  statutes on, 4–8
  time limit to the validity of a consent form, 11
  transitional living situations, patients in, 21
  withdrawal of, 13
  withholding information from a patient and, 12–13
Inhalation therapy, joint statement on, 141–142
Injection, independent liability for administration of, 102
Inoculations, consent to, 22
In re Green, 18
Insurance, professional liability, 106–107, 109
Insurance investigator or representative right of access to information about a patient, 64
Intentional wrongs, 103–104
Interdisciplinary practice issues, 79–95
  administration of medications, 92–93
  American Nurses' Association's Code of Ethics and, 82, 83
  communication of a patient's problem to appropriate other departments, 95
  "do not resuscitate" (DNR) order, 88–89
  familiarity with function and responsibility of other team members, 80
  functions and definition of nursing, 89
  guidelines on nurse's responsibility in relation to other health care professionals, 91–92
  incompetence in a health care professional other than a nurse, 95
  notification of a patient problem, physician's failure to respond to, 86–87
  nursing diagnosis differentiated from medical diagnosis, 87–88
  patient education, 90–91
  pharmacy, access to, 92
  physical therapy, 94
  physician orders, *see* Physician orders
  primary obligation to the patient or client, 90
  respiratory therapy treatments, 93–94
  tasks outside the scope of nursing practice, 89–90
Invasion-of-privacy suits, 104
Iowa, informed consent statute of, 5

Joint Commission on Accreditation of Hospitals (JCAH)
  on documentation, 51, 54–55, 58
  informed consent requirements of, 7–8
  safety standards of, 31
  "Standard of Quality Assurance" of, 27–29, 33, 35, 48–49
Joint statement
  on inhalation therapy, 141–142
  on nurse's responsibility in relation to other health care professionals, 91–92
  on standard of nursing care, 26

Index

Kelly, L., 110

Larrimore v. Homeopathic Hospital Association of Delaware, 100–101
Legal standards of care, standards of nursing care and, 39–40
Liability (Liability cases)
  documentation and, 54
  evidence in, 42–43
  independent, *see* Independent liability
  of nursing students, 123–124, 126–129
  of private duty nurses, 121–126
  proof in, 35–39
  statute of limitations, 47
  for third-party actions, 121–129
  for volunteer workers' actions, 128
  See also Negligence
Liability (Professional liability), general versus, 103
Liability insurance, 106–107, 109
Lost or damaged belongings, 104–105

McAllister, J. B., 82
Maleski, Cynthia, 132
Managerial nurses, *see* Supervisory nurses
Marcus v. Frankford Hospital, 128
Mature Minor Rule, informed consent and, 17
Medical records, 50–78
  attorney's right of access to, 63
  confidentiality of, 56, 57
  data to be included in, 58
  as evidence in liability cases, 43
  flow sheets and work sheets in, 67
  functions of, 50
  insurance investigator or representative's right of access to, 64
  as legal documents, 56–57
  letters, symbols, and abbreviations in, 71
  next-of-kin's right of access to, 61–62
  parent's right of access to, 61
  patient authorization for disclosure of information in, 58–59
  patient's request for access to, 60
  physician's right of access to, 64
  Privacy Protection Study Commission recommendations on, 59, 62–63
  right of access to, 56–64
  right to amend or add to, 62–63
  summarizing of nursing actions or observations on, 66–67
  untoward incidents in, 69
  See also Chart(ing); Recordkeeping
Medications
  administration of, 92–93, 101
  dispensing, 92
Mental institutions, informed consent of patients committed to, 21
Minors
  access to medical records of, 61
  informed consent and, 16–19
Monitoring patient's symptoms, independent liability for, 101–102
Multidisciplinary teams, *see* Interdisciplinary practice issues

National standards of care, 40–41
Negligence
  duty of affirmative action and, 42
  by other health care personnel, 127–128
  proof of, 35–39, 99
  "reasonable nursing practice" and, 41–42
  res ipsa loquitur doctrine and, 37–39

Next-of-kin consent, 19–21
Next-of-kin's right of access to medical records, 61–62
Nightingale Pledge, 82
Norton v. Argonaut Insurance Company, 101
Notes, nurses', 52–53
Notification
  of a patient problem, physician's failure to respond to, 86–87
  of potential risk problems, 76–77
Nursing, statutory definition of, 89
Nursing assistants, 129
Nursing diagnosis, 87–88
  independent liability for, 100
Nursing judgments, 97–98
Nursing Licensure Board, standard of nursing care and, 25–27
Nursing students, 123–124, 126–129
Nutrition, documentation of, 70

O'Brien v. Cunard SS Company, 2
Occupational Safety and Health Act (OSHA), 31
Oldis v. La Société Française de Bienfaisance Mutuelle, 102–103
Orders, *see* Physician orders
Orem, D. E., 52
Osteopaths, orders prescribed by 85

Parental consent, minor patients and, 16–19
Parents
  information that a minor patient does not wish revealed to, 19
  right of access to medical records, 61
Patient, nurse's primary obligation to, 90
Patient education, nurse's role in, 90–91

Patient's bill of rights, 108–109
  informed consent rules and regulations based on, 6–7
Pennsylvania
  diagnosis in, 87
  informed consent of minors in, 16–17
  informed consent statute of, 4–5
  joint statement on inhalation therapy in, 141–142
  minor's right to privacy in, 61
  pharmacist-nurse relationship in, 143–144
  professional nursing law of, 145–152
  responsibilities of the registered nurse in, 135–140
Perry, S., 110
Personnel policies and procedures, nursing supervisors and, 112
Personnel records, 77–78
Pharmacists, 92, 143–144
Photographs, consent to the taking of, 22–23
Physical therapy, 94
Physician assistants, 81
  inconsistent or conflicting standards for nurses and, 45
  orders given by, 84
Physician orders, 80–86
  for contacting a social worker, 91
  dictation of, 105
  "do not resuscitate" (DNR) order, 88–89
  independent liability for interpretation and execution of, 100–101
  nurse's responsibility in executing, 83–84
  refusal to carry out, 84–86
Physicians
  independent nursing functions and, 97
  independent nursing judgments and, 88

Index

privileged communications between patient and, 107–108
right of access to information about a patient, 64
telephone or verbal orders of, 48
See also Interdisciplinary practice issues; Physician orders
Planned Parenthood of Central Missouri v. Danforth, 22
Privacy, right to, 104, 107
Privacy Protection Study Commission, 59, 62–63
Private employer nurses, 121–126
Privileged communication, right to confidentiality and, 107–108
Professional nursing law, *see* Statutes
Professional Standards Review Organizations (PSROs), 31
Proximate causation, 36–37
Psychiatric units, informed consent of patients committed to, 21

Quality assurance program, 27–28, 48–49

Recordkeeping, 50–78
employee records, 77–78
Joint Commission on Accreditation of Hospitals' standards on, 51, 54–55, 58
nurses' notes, 52–53
See also Chart(ing); Documentation; Medical records
Refusal of treatment, 23–24
Relatives, consent of, *see* Next-of-kin consent; Parental consent, minor patients and; Spouse, informed consent of
Release form for refusal of treatment, 24
Religious beliefs, parental consent denied on the basis of, 17–18
Reporting

of clinically incorrect actions, 127–128
of inadequate staffing, 74
of incompetent or unprofessional conduct, 73–74
Res ipsa loquitur, doctrine of, 37–39
Respiratory therapists, 93–94
Respondeat superior, doctrine of, 99, 110, 112–113
Restraints, 103–104
Risk problem, notification of, 76–77

Safety standards, 31–32
Social workers, 91
Specialty unit
competence for assignment to, 105–106
temporary assignments to, 105
Spouse, informed consent of, 21–22
Staffing
quality assurance program and, 49
reporting of inadequate, 74
Standards of nursing care, 25–49
of accrediting agencies and professional associations, 27–31, 34–35
of the American Hospital Association, 29–30
American Nurses' Association, 28–30, 46–47
community versus national, 40–41
conflicting or inconsistent with standards of other professionals, 44–45
Darling decision on, 34–35
documents in a law suit concerning, 42–43
institutional policies and procedures and, 26–27

Standards (*continued*)
  of Joint Commission on the Accreditation of Hospitals, 27–29, 33, 35, 48–49
  joint statements on, 26
  legal standards of care and, 39–40
  negligence or professional liability cases and, 35–39, 47–48
  Nursing Licensure Board and, 25–27
  nursing policy and procedure manuals and, 40
  for nursing specialities, 46–47
  other health care professionals and, 44–45
  permissive and mandatory practices and, 43, 45–46
  physician's verbal or telephone orders and, 48
  policy and procedure regulations and, 39–40, 44
  reasonable nursing practice in cases of negligence, 41–42
  rules and regulations on, 25–26, 32–33, 43–44
  safety standards, 31–32
  for specific nursing functions, not addressed in a nursing practice act, 46
  for specific practice situations, 32–34, 43–44
  statutes on, 25–26, 32
"Standards of Quality Assurance," Joint Commission on the Accreditation of Hospitals, 27–29, 33, 35, 48–49
State law, *see* Statutes
Statute of limitations for liability cases, 47–48
Statutes
  definition of nursing in, 89
  good Samaritan, 110
  on informed consent, 4–8
  of Pennsylvania, 145–152
  on standard of nursing care, 25–26, 32
Supervisory nurses, 110–120
  assignment of nurses to particular units or patients by, 119–120
  departmental and institutional policies and procedures and, 119
  identification of potential or actual problems in the units supervised by, 111
  institution's hierarchy of responsibility and responsibilities of, 112–119
  personnel policies and procedures and, 112
  respondeat superior doctrine and, 112–113
  responsibility beyond the concerns of patient care, 111–112
Symbols, 71

Textbooks as evidence in a law suit, 42–43
Third-party health care workers, 121–126
Transitional living situations, informed consent of patients in, 21

Unprofessional conduct, documentation of, 72–74

Volunteer workers, 128

Warren, G., 127
Willig, S., 88
Work sheets, 67

Ybarra v. Spangard, 38, 99